Straight from the Horse's Mouth

A 60-day Devotional for Kids

Marsha Hubler

STRAIGHT FROM THE HORSE'S MOUTH BY MARSHA HUBLER
Published by Two Small Fish Publications
109 West Market Street, Freeburg, PA 17827

ISBN: 0997197280
ISBN-13: 978-0-9971972-8-0
Cover and interior design by Brenda K. Hendricks https://brendakhendricks.com
Photos by Marsha Hubler

Available in print online and from your local bookstore.

For more information about this book, horses, and the author visit:
https://horsefactsbymarshahubler.wordpress.com

Unless otherwise noted, all Scripture quotations are taken from the HOLY BIBLE
KING JAMES VERSION (KJV). Other quotations from the Bible are as follows:
the NEW KING JAMES VERSION (NKJV) and the NEW INTERNATIONAL
READER'S VERSION (NIRV).

Library of Congress Cataloging in Publication Data
 Hubler, Marsha
Straight from the Horse's Mouth/Marsha Hubler 1st ed.

Dedication

This book is dedicated to horse lovers everywhere.

Contents

Foreword

Let's Go Riding!

As a kid, I loved horses more than anything else. I've always said I was born with a silver spur in my mouth and have horse blood in my veins. I can't remember a time I didn't love horses.

If you're fortunate enough to have a horse or to be around them (like mucking stalls at a riding academy in exchange for riding lessons), then you know the thrill of climbing on a horse and jogging him around the training ring or trotting down a serene path in the woods. If you've done so, I'm sure you've treated your mount with kindness, never kicking him in the ribs too hard or slapping him in the face with your reins. In return, he's given you a wonderful ride you can talk about for hours with anyone who'll listen without yawning a lot.

When I was growing up, I lived in a small town and couldn't have a horse, but I dreamed about owning one someday. I read any horse book I could get my hands on, books such as *The Black Stallion, My Friend Flicka,* and Marguerite Henry's *Album of Horses.* I collected horse calendars, plastic horse models, and all kinds of "horse stuff." I colored horse pictures and watched TV Westerns plus any movie with horses in it. One Christmas, my parents gave me a "real" leather jacket with fringes all over it. I was in pretend horse heaven!

I finally had the chance to actually ride a horse…well, a pony. When I turned about ten, my mother took me on Sunday afternoons to a riding stable where I rode Sugar, a Shetland Pony, in a corral for half an hour at a time. Can you imagine the thrill I had every time I climbed in the saddle? I loved horses so much, I'd rub my hands real hard on Sugar when I had to get off. That way I took home with me that wonderful sweet odor of "horse." It lasted a few hours (or until my mother made me wash before eating supper.)

As I became an adult, I prayed I'd be able to have a horse of my own. I'm so happy to say that God answered my prayer. When I had my own home and a job to afford a horse or two, I had horses for a long time. I have years of wonderful "horse time" memories I'll cherish forever.

Do you know there's someone else very important in your life who loves horses as much as or more than we do?

God loves horses. Do you know there are about 150 verses in the Bible that include the word "horse?" Do you think if God mentioned equines so many times in his Holy Word that he's also very fond of one of the most beautiful creatures he ever made? But there's something, or someone, God is much fonder of than horses.

You.

God wants you to know He loves you more than anything in this world. He also wants you to know about His Son, Jesus Christ, who came to this earth over 2,000 years ago and gave His life so you could live in Heaven someday.

The best way to learn about God and Jesus is to read the Bible. We call that special quiet time with your Bible "having devotions." If you are a Christian, then you probably already have devotions every day, and that special Bible time will help you become a strong Christian with a determination to do right.

I'd like to think you've chosen to read *Straight from the Horse's Mouth* not only to learn about horses but also to learn more about our wonderful God. If you're ready for this adventure, then turn the page and learn about different breeds of horses and how they can remind you of our Savior, Jesus Christ, and your relationship with Him.

Let's saddle up and hit the trail!

> Marsha
>
> "But by the grace of God
> I am what I am..."
> (1 Corinthians 15:10a).

To see a picture of the horse featured in each devotional, go to the internet URLs listed for each horse in the back of this book.

Author's favorite horse, Rex

Day 1

The American Albino: As White as Snow

"Come now, and let us reason together, saith the LORD:
though your sins be as scarlet, they shall be as white as snow;
though they be red like crimson, they shall be as wool."
(Isaiah 1:18)

Have you ever seen a pure white horse? Ever touched one? Do you know there's a difference between an Albino and a plain white horse?

The American Albino, also called the American White, is one of the most fascinating horse breeds. It's known as a "color breed." Of course, this gorgeous animal has a white coat, white tail, and white mane. However, it's different from all other breeds because it has pink skin! If you look closely at any other breed, you'll see the skin is dark. Besides pink skin and white hair, the Albino also has black, brown, or even blue eyes.

Since this horse is a color breed, he's often seen in combination with lineage breeds like Arabians, Quarter Horses, Morgans, and

Thoroughbreds. You've probably seen American Albinos and didn't know it. They're used in movies, fairs, and circuses. You might see a white horse in a parade on TV, but the commentator says it's an Arabian. Old-time Westerns sometimes had the hero riding his white horse into the sunset. Silver, the Lone Ranger's horse, was an American Albino. Just remember, whatever the lineage breed, if the horse is white as snow, it could be an Albino too.

Do you know we can be like the American Albino and be as white as snow?

Maybe you've felt real yucky on the inside after you've done something wrong like talking back to a parent or telling a lie. Maybe you were nasty to a friend or you were lazy and didn't want to do your schoolwork or chores. Don't you just hate when you do those things, and you wish you could change?

I have super news. God's Word tells us we can change and become as white as snow. Since we can't be "good" all the time, God made a way for us to be clean on the inside in our souls. He sent His Son, Jesus, to earth to die so that anyone who believes in Him has all sin washed away. All we have to do is ask Jesus to forgive us and save us, and He will. Even after we become a Christian and do wrong and feel cruddy inside, He's ready to forgive again and again if we only ask.

If you've never asked Jesus to wash your sins away and make you white as an American Albino, there's no better time than right now. We can't get to Heaven by being good. No one is *that* good. It's only because Christ's perfect blood washes us white as snow that we can go to Heaven when we die. Ask Jesus to save you, and you'll forever be glad you did. Whenever you see an Albino, you can think of the special day you asked Jesus to come into your life and make you as white as snow.

PRAYER:

Dear God, I'm sorry for all my sins, especially when I have a bad attitude. Today I want Jesus to save me and make me ready for Heaven. I accept Him as my personal Savior. I know He can make me as white as snow on my inside. Show me how to become a better person and how to choose the right things. Thank you. In Jesus' name, amen.

SADDLE UP!   (What would God have you do now?)

If you've asked Jesus to save you, do you think you should tell anyone?

If you don't go to church, do you think God would want you to go? Would anyone be glad to take you? Write their names here:

_____

_____

Take your ride: (Do you know?)

Although white horses are sometimes called "albino," there are no reported cases of a true albino horse. The absence of pigment cells called melanocytes causes the white color. All so-called albino horses have pigmented eyes, generally brown or blue. In contrast, many albino mammals, such as mice or rabbits, have white hair, unpigmented skin, and reddish eyes. Despite this issue, some registries still refer to albino horses.

Dismount and cool down your horse! (Do you know?)

"For God so loved the world, that he gave his only begotten Son, that whosoever believeth in him should not perish, but have everlasting life" (John 3:16).

Day 2

The Abtenauer: Small but Mighty

*"For the weapons of our warfare are not carnal, but mighty
through God to the pulling down of strong holds."*
(2 Corinthians 10:4)

If you're a horse lover and live in the country of Austria, you probably know what an Abtenauer horse is. An Abtenauer is a small stocky horse many folks think is just a pony. That's because the breed's average height is only 14 to 15 hands. (A "hand" measures about four inches.) This cute lineage breed comes from a special place in Austria, an isolated valley called the Abtenauer, tucked away in the beautiful Alps Mountains not far from Salzburg.

Abtenauers, known as "draft horses" (those that pull heavy loads), are extremely strong for their size, but they have a sweet temperament and enjoy working with humans. Therefore, their labor mostly involves pulling wagons like buckboards loaded with people or harvested crops. Some Abtenauers also work in the forest, pulling huge tree trunks for loggers.

Foals are born with curly hair and are black, blue roan (a dark coat with white hairs speckled throughout), brown, or chestnut. When the foals shed their first coat, the curls disappear, and they have straight hair from then on.

Because this little breed is confined to such a small part of the world, their number has become low, maybe as few as a hundred or so. Yet, in the Abtenauer Valley, they are quite popular and are celebrated for their stamina.

How can such a small horse have such strength to pull a wagon full of people or heavy bags of grain? If you ask me, that job takes a lot of determination!

God has given the Abtenauer an elegant build with a well-shaped head and strong legs full of muscles that allow this little horse to power up and trot with an easy flow. The Abtenauer truly is mighty, not only for his conformation but for his "I can do this" attitude!

Do you ever feel badly because you're small in stature or you feel "small" because you struggle with your studies? Maybe you're the tiniest one in your family or in your circle of friends. Does that mean you can't do the same things other kids do or get good grades? Do you ever say, "I can't do that. I'm too little"? Do you ever think it?

God tells us in His Bible the size of a person doesn't matter to Him. In fact, God has made you the way you are. Of course, if you're short, you might not be able to win at basketball or a high jump event, but God has other plans for you. Whether you're short or thin, God loves you, and you can be mighty in whatever tasks He asks you to do.

Are you too short to help your mother dust the furniture or dry the dishes? Are you too short to get an A in that math test? Are you too short to tell someone "I love you?" I think the answer should be "I can do this!"

In Luke chapter 19, the Bible tells of a man named Zacchaeus, who wanted to meet Jesus. Zacchaeus was so short, he couldn't see over the crowd. But he didn't whimper like a lost puppy and go home. Instead, he said, "I can do this!" He climbed the nearest tree, met Jesus, and became a mighty witness for God. Zacchaeus didn't use his puny height as an excuse not to serve God.

How about you? Are you shy or maybe a little clumsy? Whether you're small in stature or feel small inside, you can be mighty for God. Ask God to give you strength you never knew you had to do the job He's asked you to do. There's no better time than right now to make up your mind to be a mighty warrior for God. Ask Him to help you to always have an "I can do it" attitude, and you'll be amazed at all you can achieve for the Lord Jesus Christ.

You might be small, but you can still be mighty!

PRAYER:

Dear God, Sometimes I feel so small and weak. I pray you will help me have an "I can do this" attitude for anything you ask me to do. I am willing. Please make me mighty with your power. Thank you. In Jesus' name, amen.

SADDLE UP! (What would God have you do now?)

To learn more about our wonderful God, try to read your Bible every day. You could ask for a children's Bible to help you understand it better.

Start reading the book of John in the New Testament. Write a verse from the book of John that you really like:

_____

_____

_____

_____

Take your ride: (Do you know?)

When the Abtenauers aren't working, they're grazing, sometimes with cows, in lush pastures in the beautiful Abtenauer Valley.

Dismount and cool down your horse: (Do you know?)

"I can do all things through Christ who strengthens me" (Philippians 4:13 NKJV).

Day 3

The Akhal-teke: Shines like the Stars

"And they that be wise shall shine as the brightness of the firmament; and they that turn many to righteousness as the stars for ever and ever."
(Daniel 12:3)

If you've heard of the Akhal-Teke (AH-kuhl TEH-kee), then you are a true horse lover who's interested in learning all about equines. Most folks, even some horse enthusiasts, have never heard of this breed.

The Akhal-Teke is one of the most stunning horses God ever created. If you've ever seen one in person or even in a photo, you might have thought someone had sprayed this amazing animal with metallic paint, no matter what the horse's color. How did he get his spectacular appearance? Our creative God gave this horse's coat a gorgeous metallic sheen that almost glitters.

To say the Akhal-Teke is a rare breed is an understatement. It's believed to be one of the oldest and purest breeds, originating from Russia and Turkmenistan (countries in Asia), where most are found today. At last count, there were only about 6,500 of these beauties world-wide with about 500 in North America.

When you look at an Akhal-Teke, you might think he's so delicate, he can't do anything but stand around and look pretty. But that's not the case. This horse has proven himself not only in dressage (dres-sahg´- a highly-skilled form of riding performed in competition) but also in "tough" competitions like fox hunting and extreme trail riding. But what catches everyone's eye is not the horse's performance. It's the shiny coat.

Akhal-Tekes can have any solid color of undercoat, but the natural metallic sheen shows best in lighter colors like cremello (cream). In fact, palomino and buckskin Akhal-Tekes are so beautiful, they're nicknamed "Golden Horses." In the sun, they shine almost as bright as the stars on a crystal, clear night. Whether an Akhal-Teke is performing in a circus or prancing in a parade, all heads turn toward the horse with the sparkling coat.

If you are a Christian, do you ever wonder how you can "shine for Jesus?" Maybe when you were little, you sang "This Little Light of Mine." What do you think that means?

Shining for Jesus is something any Christian can do. You might think you're still too young to do anything that would make you "shine," but that's not the case. Even at your age, you can please God by having a good attitude. That's being wise. You can also help around the house and listen to your Sunday school teacher and pastor in church. Being a good example is the best way to "shine like the stars." Ask God to help you be a good example to others and give you the courage to talk to your friends about Jesus. Some day in Heaven, you'll shine as bright as the stars!

Jesus, the Bright and Morning Star, will help you every step of the way.

PRAYER:

Dear God, please help me to be wise and have the courage to talk to my friends about you. I want them to know Jesus as their Savior. And I would love to shine like the stars when I meet you face to face. Thank you. In Jesus' name, amen.

SADDLE UP! (What would God have you do now?)

It's a good idea to have an attitude check every day.
Have you ever told any of your friends about Jesus? Write the names of the friends you'd like to tell about Jesus:

_____

_____

Take your ride: (Do you know?)

Because the Akhal-Teke has been crossbred so much with the Thoroughbred to create a fast, long-distance racehorse, all Akhal-

Tekes have Thoroughbred blood in them.

Dismount and cool down your horse! (Do you know?)

"Let your light so shine before men, that they may see your good works, and glorify your Father which is heaven" (Matthew 5:16).

Author on Rex a long time ago

Day 4

The American Paint:
A Horse of a Different Color

"Thy Word have I hid in my heart, that I might not sin against thee." (Ps.119:11)

The American Paint Horse is a splashy equine that turns heads in his direction. When a Paint prances by, the onlookers will stand in awe because of the horse's stunning colors.

You might think, *Oh, I know all about Pintos. They're spotted horses.* That idea is a common error because Paints and Pintos are two separate breeds. (We'll discuss Pintos much later.)

The American Paint Horse is a western stock horse (has a husky, muscular build) that stands between 14.2 and 16.2 hands with spots or "patches" of white and dark colors and must have either Quarter Horse or Thoroughbred parents. Also, because that horse must have a specific body shape and size to be registered, the American Paint Horse is a "horse" (lineage) breed as well as a color breed. It's not surprising that Paints are one of the most popular horses in the United States.

So, where did Paints get their start?

The first known record of any "two-colored" horses in America happened in 1519, when the Spanish explorer Hernando Cortes brought two horses described as having pinto markings on his voyage. Somehow over time, probably by trading, the flashy horses became favorites of Native Americans, in particular, the Comanche tribe. (Paint horses have been found in drawings sketched or sewn on buffalo robes.) By the early 1800s, horses with paint coloring were well-populated throughout the West.

Throughout the 1800s and into the mid-1900s, the two-or-three-toned horses were called pinto, paint, skewbald (any brown or blond with white) and piebald (black and white). In the early 1960s, interest grew in preserving and promoting horses with paint coloring and stock horse builds, so in 1965 the American Paint Horse Association formed. Today, you'll find the American Paint Horse in practically every traditional stock-horse western competition as well as a variety of other riding events.

Most Paints are a splashy combination of either black and white or different shades of brown and white. Over the years, so many different combinations of colors have been bred that the American Paint Horse Association divided Paints into two different categories: overo and tobiano. The best way to remember the difference is that tobianos look like white horses that have been "painted" with brown spots. Overos look like dark horses with white patches painted on their coats. Whether marching in a parade or just jogging down a wooded trail, this spotted horse with his dashing variety of colors always draws smiles from so many fans. He's certainly a horse of a different color!

Do you have friends who think you are "different?" If you're a Christian, who's not ashamed to tell others about Jesus, some people might think you *are* different. Do you agree to do good deeds and help others? Do you say no when someone suggests you do something against what God would want you to do? If you've made up your mind to stand for Christ and live for him, then you can be just like the American Paint Horse and be a "horse of a different color."

PRAYER:

Dear God, please help me to be different for you when I'm around those who want to do wrong. Give me the courage to say yes to what's right and no to what's wrong. Thank you. In Jesus' name, amen.

SADDLE UP! (What would God have you do now?)

Are there some activities you know God would not want you to do with your friends? Write those activities here and ask God to help you say no:

_____

_____

_____

_____

Take your ride: (Do you know?)

Paint horses with black spots are called "piebalds." Paints with any other colored spots are called "skewbalds."

Dismount and cool down your horse! (Do you know?)

"This righteousness from God comes through faith in Jesus Christ to all who believe. There is no difference" (Romans 3:22 NIRV).

Day 5

The American Quarter Horse:
Fast as Lightning

"For as the lightning cometh out of the east, and shineth even unto the west; so shall also the coming of the Son of man be."
(Matthew 24:27)

This little equine isn't a quarter of a horse. He's all horse, and he's an All-American!

Way, way back in the late 1700s, the colonists in Virginia met a new kind of a horse, one as fast as lightning. The stocky, muscular horse was a cross between Mustangs, which Native Americans rode, and the English horses brought to the New World in earlier years. The small sturdy horse came in any color or combination of colors. Quick, smart, and eager to work, he captivated the hearts of the colonists. But working hard didn't attract the horse's fancy as much as racing.

In early colonial days, race tracks didn't exist, so the colonists made their own "track," clearing out a straight, flat stretch of land about a quarter-mile long. The new horse on the block amazed everyone by achieving speeds of up to 55 miles per hour over that short stint. Beyond that distance, the Thoroughbred always won. But because of the little horse's dominance of the quarter mile track, he became known as the Quarter Horse.

With his eager yet gentle nature, the Quarter Horse has become one of the most popular riding horses in America. Early Americans discovered the breed worked well on the farm and seemed to have a natural instinct for working around cattle. So, in the 1800s when the settlers began migrating to the West, the Quarter Horse became the choice of the early cowboys for ranching and cattle roundups. Before long, rodeos emerged as a popular pastime, and cowboys soon realized the little Quarter Horse excelled at events like calf roping and barrel racing. The horse became so predominant, a group of horsemen and ranchers formed the American Quarter Horse Association in 1940 and made the special equine his own breed.

Today, the Quarter Horse has won the hearts of horse lovers all over the world. With about five million registered in America alone, it's no wonder the American Quarter Horse is the number one breed in the United States. Who wouldn't want to own a stocky, little horse with a gentle nature but fast as lightning?

Speaking of lightning, there are at least a dozen verses in the Bible about lightning. One of the most encouraging verses is found in the book of Matthew that tells us Jesus is going to come back to earth someday for everyone who believes in Him as Savior. He'll come as fast as lightning and call all Christians to meet him in the air and go with him to Heaven. The Bible tells us to always be ready to meet Jesus and to keep looking for His return.

What about you? Do you know Jesus is coming back again for everyone who believes in Him? Are you anxious to see Jesus face to face?

There's one way to be ready. If you're a Christian, keep looking up and watch for Jesus to come as fast as lightning!

PRAYER:

Dear God, please forgive me when I sin and give in to temptation. I want to be ready to meet you when you come for us Christians. Thank you. In Jesus' name, amen.

SADDLE UP! (What would God have you do now?)

Write any sin or wrong doing that seems to trouble you and you find hard to give up. More than one? Maybe it's time to ask God to forgive you and help you fight the temptation.

_____

_____

_____

Take your ride: (Do you know?)

Although Quarter Horses can come in any color or combination of colors, the most prominent color is sorrel (reddish brown) or chestnut.

Dismount and cool down your horse! (Do you know?)

"For the Lord himself shall descend from heaven with a shout, with the voice of the archangel, and with the trump of God: and the dead in Christ shall rise first: Then we which are alive and remain shall be caught up together with them in the clouds, to meet the Lord in the air: and so shall we ever be with the Lord" *(1Thessalonians 4:16-17).*

Day 6

The American Saddlebred:
Proud as a Peacock!

"...God resists the proud, but gives grace to the humble."
(James 4:6b NKJV)

If you want a flashy, high-stepping show horse and you have the money to buy one, then you want an American Saddlebred, also known as the Saddle Horse or Kentucky Saddler. This horse has class!

By now, you've probably figured that the word "American" tagged to a horse's official name means the horse had his origins in the United States. Such is true of the American Saddlebred. For a long time in his history, this breed was referred to as "the horse America made." Starting with riding horses during the American Revolution, he has roots with the Morgan, Narragansett Pacer, Canadian Pacer, and Thoroughbred.

Throughout the 20th Century, the breed became popular in

the United States, and since the formation of the U.S. registry in 1891, almost 250,000 American Saddlebreds have been registered. Today the Saddlebred can be found in countries all around the world, and breed registries exist in Great Britain, Australia, Europe, and southern Africa.

The Saddlebred is a "taller" slim horse, averaging 15 to 16 hands (60 to 64 inches) in height. When this spunky equine prances into the show ring, he oozes a sense of presence and style. Although the Saddlebreds are very spirited, the breed is known for its gentle temperament. They may be of any color, including pinto patterns accepted since the late 1800s.

Something quite different about the Saddlebred is that's it's a "gaited" breed. Does that mean they have to be kept in fences with strong gates? Not so.

A "gait" is a step. Saddlebreds show in three-gaited or five-gaited classes, depending on the different speeds or steps each horse has. Saddlebreds are mainly known for their performance in the show ring, but they can enter hunter and driving classes, as well as just being a fantastic pleasure riding horse.

If you ever own an American Saddlebred, you might want to show him in one of five divisions: Five-Gaited, Three-Gaited, Fine Harness, Park, and Pleasure. In those divisions they are judged on performance, presence, quality, and conformation. But one thing is for sure. Whatever gait the horse is performing, he's high-stepping it. No wonder he's now called "the Peacock of the Horse World."

Have you ever felt proud as a peacock about anything you've done or anything you might own? Do you brag about new stuff your parents buy you? Maybe you think your house is better than all your friends' houses. Maybe you look in the mirror and think you're the best-looking kid on the block.

"Is that a bad attitude?" you might ask.

The Bible says quite a bit about being proud of the wrong things. If you're proud, thinking you've done something great or because of something you own or the way you look, God wants us to know that's the wrong pride. He wants us to develop a humble, or respectful, opinion about others, especially about Him. A respectful person puts others first in his life and looks to serve them.

But you might be thinking, *I'm proud to be a Christian. Is that wrong?*

If you're proud to be a Christian, it's a good thing as long as you don't gloat. To gloat means to feel smug or better than someone else. It's important to let others know you are a Christian, but when you act like you're better than others, they probably won't be interested when you want to tell them about Jesus. It's much better to develop a sweet, helping attitude that others will love about you. Then they might want to know why you're so different, and you can tell them all about your wonderful Savior.

PRAYER:

Dear God, help me not to brag or be proud of the wrong things. Help me to have a humble, helpful spirit. Thank you. In Jesus' name, amen.

SADDLE UP! (What would God have you do now?)

Can you think of any time you might have had the wrong kind of pride about something? Write it here and ask God to forgive you and help you develop a humble spirit:

_____

_____

_____

_____

Take your ride: (Do you know?)

Saddlebred horses that have won a lot of shows can cost $30,000 or more.

Dismount and cool down your horse! (Do you know?)

"When pride cometh, then cometh shame: but with the lowly is wisdom"
(Proverbs 11:2).

Day 7

The American Warmblood:
Not a Cold Spot in His Heart

"Let my heart be blameless regarding Your statutes,
That I may not be ashamed."
(Psalm 119:80 NKJV)

Here's another American original with his roots as late as the 1980s! The American Warmblood is usually between 15 and 17 hands high, weighs 1,350 pounds, which is 325 pounds heavier than the average horse breed, and may come in any color, although the solid colors are most common. All kinds of horses can be registered as American Warmbloods as long as they are of a sport horse or warmblood type. No pure hotbloods or coldbloods can be included in this exclusive club. So what is a "warmblood type?" And how about a hotblood and a coldblood?

If you go shopping for an American Warmblood, you'd look for a horse that has the registry standards of three different breeds:

draft horses (coldbloods), Arabians, and Thoroughbreds (both hotbloods).

Let's take a time-out and make sure we understand the difference between coldbloods and hotbloods.

Coldbloods are your power horses, those big guys who pull really heavy loads like tree trunks for loggers, plow fields, or plod with a stagecoach behind them in a parade. "The Big Four of the Draft World," Belgians, Percherons, Shires, and Clydesdales, have the reputation of not only strength but also a laid-back, gentle disposition.

Hotbloods like the Arabians and Thoroughbreds are the complete opposite. They're super eager to run fast, have a high-spirited temperament, and, although they're loyal, can be spooked easily. Hotbloods set their sights on the finish line and chafe at the bit to get there.

Now, back to our Warmblood. He has no major health issues and is usually alert, calm yet energetic and obedient. In other words, he's just a nice guy. He's also a multi-tasker. You might buy this breed to ride in dressage, general riding, jumping, or mounted athletics activities; yet, the breed is a very popular draft horse seen in harness in parades and show competitions.

Wow, a horse so trustworthy, you can sit in a wagon and let him pull you around the countryside or down a noisy street in a parade? There's a reason he's called a Warmblood. He's tender, and he aims to please the folks who love him. In fact, he doesn't have a cold spot anywhere in his heart.

How about you? Would your friends and family consider you "warm-blooded?" Are you kind and gentle to those around you, or are you a complainer? Do you try your best to please others, or do you lose your temper when you don't get your own way?

The Warmblood has a "warm" servant's heart and wants to do the best job he can. Maybe you never thought about the condition of your heart before. If it's warm, you'll try hard to please your family and friends, and with a good attitude. However, if there's a cold spot in your heart, big or small, perhaps it's time to ask God to help you get rid of anything in your heart that would cause you to disappoint Him and others. The best way to start is to read and study God's Word. Then God can change you from the inside out.

PRAYER:

Dear God, please help me to have a warm heart toward others. Help me to love my family and friends and put their interests ahead of mine. Thank you. In Jesus' name, amen.

SADDLE UP! (What would God have you do now?)

List some things you could do for your family and friends to show them and God you have a "warm" heart:

_____

_____

_____

_____

Take your ride: (Do you know?)

Hot-blooded horses have light bodies and a passion to run, ideal for racing. But they're often high strung or fiery tempered. Thoroughbreds and Arabians are the only hot-blooded breeds. Cold bloods are large, gentle horses used for farming, hauling, and other heavy work. Friesians and Haflingers are members of that family.

Dismount and cool down your horse! (Do you know?)

"Search me, O God, and know my heart: try me, and know my thoughts: And see if there be any wicked way in me, and lead me in the way everlasting" (Psalms *139:23-24).*

Day 8

The Andalusian: Fit for a King

"Hearken unto the voice of my cry, my King, and my God: for unto thee will I pray."
(Psalm 5:2)

The Andalusian horse is a real beauty, standing between 15 and 16.2 hands. This breed is most often gray or bay (a shade of brown with a black mane, black tail, and often black legs below the knee), but once in a while you might see a black or chestnut Andalusian prancing by. He's well built with a finely sculptured head, alert ears, lively yet kind eyes, an elegant arched neck, and a long and often wavy mane and tail.

This breed descended from the horses of Spain and Portugal and derives its name from Andalusia, a region in southern Spain, where his ancestors lived for thousands of years. He's also known as the Pure Spanish Horse or P.R.E. (Pura Raza Española).

This magnificent breed has been recognized since the 15th Century, and his conformation has changed very little over the centuries. From the very beginning, Andalusians have been used for both riding and driving. Among the first horses used for dressage, they're still making a mark in that international competition today.

The Andalusian has always been known for his incredible athletic ability as a war horse. The Quarter Horse and other breeds noted for their "cow sense" inherited that ability from their Andalusian ancestors. (Horses with "cow sense" are good at anticipating the next move of cattle they are trying to corner or single out of a herd, particularly to cutting horses. They seem to understand cattle and can almost read their minds.)

Also, bull owners gave the Andalusian his reputation as the greatest athlete and stock-working animal in the equine world. In Spain, cowboys have long used them in handling the bulls, which can be quite ornery. Many other horse breeds run the opposite direction from these dangerous animals; yet, Andalusians seem to delight in confronting a nasty bull. With the incredible speed, they can maneuver quickly, dodging in and out and barely missing the hooking horns when the bull charges.

Andalusian blood has had a strong influence on almost every breed in ancient times. But most interesting is the fact that Andalusians became a favorite for kings and knights, mostly because of the horse's regal high step. Although the Andalusian has always been expensive, a wealthy knight would never be found plodding along on a lazy, low-headed mount. The prancing Andalusian had to have an arched neck to be chosen to carry royalty.

It's no surprise this horse is nicknamed "The Horse of Kings." The breed was so respected, a quote spoken over 300 years ago by William Cavendish, Duke of Newcastle, has also stood the tests of time: "... the noblest horse in the world, the most beautiful that can be. He is of great spirit and of great courage and docile; hath the proudest trot and the best action in his trot, the loftiest gallop, and is the lovingest and gentlest horse, and fittest of all for a king in his day of triumph."[1] The Andalusian truly is a horse fit for a king!

How about you? Are you fit for a king?

"Fit for a king?" you might say. "I've never even met a king or a president. How can I be fit for a king?"

I'm talking about the King of kings and Lord of lords, the Lord Jesus Christ. Are you "fit" for that King?

The Bible says when we accept Jesus as our Savior, He becomes the "King" of our lives. Subjects who love their king (or leader) try to please him with their good deeds and loyalty. If you're a young Christian, your desire should be to please God with everything you do and say.

Are you sure that activity you want to do will please God? The best way to serve your King is to read His Bible, go to church, and pray. Ask God for His guidance, and He'll help you every day.

---

[1] https://en.wikipedia.org/wiki/Andalusian_horse

PRAYER:

Dear God, I want to please you and honor you as my King. Help me to always remember I serve the King of kings and Lord of lords and that I want to be a faithful follower of you. Thank you. In Jesus' name, amen.

SADDLE UP! (What would God have you do now?)

Write three things you could do that would show Jesus that He's the King of your life.

_____

_____

_____

Take your ride: (Do you know?)

The Iberian and Celtiberian soldiers of the famous Carthaginian horse troops used magnificent Andalusians to carry the Roman army in its conquests throughout the ancient world.

Dismount and cool down your horse! (Do you know?)

"Now unto the King eternal, immortal, invisible, the only wise God, be honour and glory for ever and ever. Amen" (1 Timothy 1: 17).

Day 9

The Appaloosa:
A Blanket of Brilliance

"Blessed is he whose transgression is forgiven, whose sin is covered."
(Psalm 32:1)

The splashy Appaloosa is one of the most popular breeds in the United States, so popular it was even named the official state horse of Idaho in 1975. The breed as we know it today is believed to have originated in the northwestern Native American tribe called the Nez Perce way back in the 17th Century. But did this horse get his earliest start in other parts of the world?

Some French cave paintings thousands of years old show "spotted" horses like Appaloosas. In China, the ancient peoples called this horse "heavenly," and Persians have called him "sacred." But here in the westward expansion of our American territory, the colonists first noticed the beautiful breed as the favorite horse of a unique people, who lived near the Palouse River (which runs from north central Idaho to the Snake River in southeast Washington

State.) The Nez Perce Indians rode stunning equines with spots all over their rumps. The pioneers had never seen anything like this breed of horse that stood between 14 and 16 hands. They started calling him "palousey," which means "the stream of the green meadows." Eventually, the name changed to "Appaloosa."

People who don't know much about horses often confuse Appaloosas with Pintos, thinking they are the same, but they certainly aren't. Although "Apps" are known for the blankets on their rumps, there are ten different patterns of spots found on Appaloosas. They can have spots all over their dark or light-colored bodies. But an App must also have some characteristics quite unique to be registered as an official pureblood Appaloosa: striped hooves, spotted skin around his eyes and lips, and a white outer coat called a sclera encircling his brown or blue eyes.

If you want to buy a gorgeous Appaloosa mare and her foal, you might be surprised to see the foal with a solid coat. Therefore, it's not always easy to predict a grown App's color at birth. Spot patterns emerge over time but sometimes change over the course of the horse's life. Apps with a varnish roan or snowflake pattern are two that become more visible as they grow. Some horses, like those with the blanket or leopard patterns, tend to stay the same once their spots start to emerge. But one thing is certain. The blanket or "covering" of the Appaloosa makes this husky stock horse a head turner whether he's competing in western horse shows, strolling down the street in a parade, or ambling on a woodsy trail.

The covering of the Appaloosa makes him a special horse. Do you have a "covering" in your life that makes you special to God?

This covering we call "salvation" is the one God places over every person who accepts Jesus Christ as his or her Savior. Like a blanket smothering the flames of a destructive fire, God places his covering of love over our sins and smothers them when Jesus comes into our lives and gives us the desire and power to do right.

Do you have God's covering of love in your life? If you do, then when you struggle with anger, being nasty, or laziness and say you're sorry, God's ready to forgive you and cover you with His love. And when you walk by, others will notice a "blanket of brilliance" that comes from your smiling face and servant's heart.

PRAYER:

Dear God, thank you for covering my sins and giving me a new way of thinking. Please help me to display my "blanket of brilliance" to others. In Jesus' name, amen.

SADDLE UP!   (What would God have you do now?)

Write some bad habits God is helping you overcome since He's covered your sins:

_____

_____

_____

_____

_____

Take your ride: (Do you know?)

Roan is a coat pattern with an even mixture of colored and white hairs on the horse with his head, lower legs, mane, and tail mostly solid colors. The silvering effect of mixed white and colored hairs often creates coats that look bluish or pinkish. Bluish roans are called "blue roans," and pinkish roans are called "strawberry roans" or "red roans."

Dismount and cool down your horse! (Do you know?)

"Hatred stirs up strife, but love covers all sins" (Proverbs 10:12 NKJV).

Day 10

The Arabian:
"The China Doll of the Horse Kingdom"

"Moreover it is required in stewards, that a man be found faithful."
(1 Corinthians 4:2)

There's not a horse lover anywhere who doesn't drool when gazing at one of the most perfect creatures in the Animal Kingdom. Sometimes called "The China Doll of the Horse Kingdom," the Arabian is known as an absolutely stunning horse because of his delicate features. Researchers have long believed this breed is the oldest and purest. It's not known for sure if he originated in Arabia, but evidence found in archaeological digs dates the Arabian back 4,500 years.

Bible scholars believe the first horse God created in the Garden of Eden must have had the traits of strength and beauty seen in the Arabian today. It's also a rarely debated fact that all other horse breeds descended from this gorgeous breed that also has stamina, courage, and intelligence.

A purebred Arabian is small in stature, only 14 or 15 hands. But don't let his size fool you. He has strong endurance to tough circumstances and is extremely loyal to his rider. Other features that catch the eye of horse lovers include a delicate "dish" face with a broad forehead and tiny muzzle, two alert ears, and large eyes that often have rings of black. He also has a graceful, arched neck and a high carriage in his tail. The breed can come in practically any color, including dappled and some paint, but you can know for sure if the horse is of Arabian blood if you run your finger against the grain of his coat and see an underlying bed of black skin. If that's the case, then even an Arabian who might appear to be white is called a "gray."

If you think you'd like to own an Arabian, it's recommended that you have riding experience. Arabians, as gorgeous and loyal as they are, have a reputation of being high-spirited even after they're well-trained and ridden for years. Your Arabian might take you on a ride you'll never forget!

Many horse lovers think the combination of loyalty and high-spiritedness is a tremendous asset in any breed of horse. But are they two traits a Christian young person also should have in his or her life?

How about you? Do you consider yourself loyal to anything? To anyone?

Another word for loyal is "faithful." A faithful Christian wants to please God by attending church, reading his Bible, and praying. A faithful young person will also stand up for God at school or with friends. Do you stand up for God or are you ashamed you are a Christian?

Do you consider yourself high-spirited?

One definition of "high-spirited" is to be lively and full of fun. If you're full of fun and pleasant when others are around, you're the best kind of high-spirited person. Everyone loves someone who has joy in his or her heart and wants to do right, no matter the circumstances.

So, if you want to be like the classy Arabian, determine to be faithful to God. Work hard to develop an excitement deep in your soul to do right and make up your mind to smile while you're doing it.

PRAYER:

Dear God, please help me to be faithful and joyful in my church attendance, Bible reading, and prayer. I want to please you in everything I do. In Jesus' name, amen.

SADDLE UP! (What would God have you do now?)

Are there any chores you must do that make it hard for you to be faithful when doing them? Do you do them with a joyful spirit? Write the chores here and tell how you can improve:

_____

_____

_____

_____

_____

Take your ride: (Do you know?)

The Arabian is classified as a hot-blooded breed, a category that includes delicate, spirited horses bred for speed.

Dismount and cool down your horse! (Do you know?)

"And my soul shall be joyful in the Lord: it shall rejoice in his salvation" (Psalm 35:9).

Day 11

The Australian Brumby:
Free as the Wind

*"For the law of the Spirit of life in Christ Jesus has
made me free from the law of sin and death."*
(Romans 8:2)

What the Mustang is to the United States, the Brumby is to Australia.

The Brumby is a free-roaming feral horse in The Land Down Under. The word "feral" refers to animals that live in the wild after having been domesticated by humans. The best-known Brumbies are found in the southeast Australian Alps, although herds of them are found in many areas of the country. Most of them roam freely in the Northern Territory in one of the largest herds in Queensland.

Although we would say a group of horses is a herd, a group of Brumbies is known as a "mob" or "band." Brumbies are the descendants of escaped or lost horses, probably dating back to the late1700s. They crossbred with steeds of European settlers, horses from South Africa, Timor Ponies from Indonesia, British ponies and draught (draft) horses, and a large number of Thoroughbreds and

Arabians. With all that cross-breeding, today the Brumby just looks like your average horse, usually solid colored and stocky.

The first report of an escaped horse in Australia was in 1804. But by the 1840s, it was common knowledge the horses were escaping from settled regions. Perhaps fences were not properly installed, if fences existed at all! Actually, it's believed that most Australian horses became feral because they were released into the wild and left to fend for themselves. That might have happened when some ranchers abandoned their settlements due to extremely dry conditions and harsh lands, making farming too difficult.

It's estimated that at least 400,000 horses roam Australia. Wow! That's a lot of wild horses! Feral horses are considered a moderate pest because they sometimes wander on ranches where they damage vegetation and cause erosion. During drought conditions, they eat the already threatened and limited vegetation and chew the bark off trees. Therefore, trying to manage the large herds has become a complicated issue between ranchers and the government. Unfortunately, being free to run doesn't offer the best situation for the Brumbies.

Today thousands of Brumbies live in designated national parks in Australia. Sadly over the years, because there were so many wild horses, the government shot thousands until the public outcry convinced agents to use other means to control the herds. Adoption centers have been established. Occasionally the Brumbies are rounded up and domesticated for use as camp drafters, stock horses on farms, trail horses, show horses, Pony Club mounts, and pleasure horses. High-risk youth (children who have gotten into some kind of trouble with the law) benefit by attending training camps where they work with Brumbies, training them to become safe trail horses.

An exciting time for Brumbies is a catch-and-handle event in stockman's challenge competitions held throughout the year. Riders on horseback must catch a running Brumby within a time limit of a few minutes. Points are awarded for the cowboys' skill in catching the Brumby and their ability to teach them to lead. The most famous event is probably the "Man from Snowy River Challenge" in Corryong, Victoria, because of the popularity of two movies, *The Man from Snowy River* and *The Man from Snowy River II*.

Australians are proud of their horse breed's heritage of running wild. Horse enthusiasts work hard to keep the Brumby bands free. If you had the opportunity to ask a Brumby what he'd like, I'm sure he'd say the same thing: "I love running free as the wind."

When you think of Brumbies running free across the mountains and plains of Australia, do you wish you could be one of those horses and run wild and free? Well, there is a way that every boy and girl can be "free," much more than even the Brumbies.

The Bible tells us that every person since the beginning of time has had the ability, and often the desire, to sin. Those sins make us feel ashamed. But when we accept Christ as our Savior, the bad feelings and guilt of doing those wrong things are wiped away, and we can feel free as the wind in our souls. Even after we become Christians, we can mess up, but that's the time to ask Christ to forgive us. We then can feel free to start living for Him again and trying to please him every day. All it takes is our sincere prayer, admitting the things we've done wrong.

Do you want to be free as those Brumbies? Be determined to do right in every situation and pray for forgiveness when you do mess up. God is willing to forgive and set you free again.

PRAYER:

Dear God, sometimes I don't feel free at all when sin nags me and keeps me tied down. Please help me to forsake the sin, so I can feel free as the wind. In Jesus' name, amen.

SADDLE UP!   (What would God have you do now?)

List any sins that hold you back from feeling free. Then write what you can do to rid them from your life.

_____

_____

_____

_____

_____

Take your ride: (Do you know?)

The Brumby was adopted as an emblem in 1996 by a rugby union team called the ACT Brumbies from Canberra, Australia.

Dismount and cool down your horse! (Do you know?)

"It is for freedom that Christ has set us free. Stand firm, then, and do not let yourselves be burdened again by a yoke of slavery" (Galatians 5:1 NIRV).

Day 12

The Austrian Warmblood: A Loyal "Soldier"

"Thou therefore endure hardness, as a good soldier of Jesus Christ."
(2 Timothy 2:3)

The Austrian Warmblood comes from Austria, a country in Europe, long known for its outstanding horses. Like other Warmbloods, this stunning steed was developed as a super riding and competition horse. He has his roots in old Austrian cavalry (war) horses combined with the delicate Arabian and Warmblood sport horses, namely the Nonius and Furioso, both from Hungary.

In the mid-19th Century, the war horse/sport horse combination was crossed with Thoroughbreds and more Arabians to further refine the breed. And what a beauty emerged! From those came a horse suitable for classy dressage and show jumping as well as for trail riding.

Like many breeds in the mid-20th Century, the rise of machines, especially the automobile, caused the numbers of

Warmbloods to decline. However to save the breed, Warmblood enthusiasts in Austria founded an organization in 1964 called the Association for Warmblood Breeding to promote the horse. Even so, the breed is still "battling" for recognition. It's estimated only about 800 Austrian Warmbloods exist today.

This handsome horse has a height from 15.2 to 16.2 hands. Although solid colors of chestnut, gray, bay, and black are most desirable, a pinto studbook has been approved. (A studbook is a list of approved stallions available for breeding.)Whatever his color, the Austrian Warmblood has the reputation of having a pleasant character and a balanced temperament. If you see a Warmblood in action today, you'd never think this splashy mount could have been a warrior in battle hundreds of years ago, but that's a fact.

The Warmblood has a history of being a good "soldier," starting out in the Austrian cavalry. He had the reputation of being very loyal to his rider. Loyalty to the leader defines a good soldier.

How about you? Would you consider yourself a good soldier?

"I'm not in any army," you might say. "How can I be a soldier?"

The Bible talks about Christians being good soldiers of Jesus Christ. If you love the Lord with all your heart, you'll strive to be a good soldier by obeying God's Word and doing the best you can every day. If you live to please God, then you are a good soldier. As you work hard to that end, remember to get your marching orders from the Bible, and you'll be a loyal and faithful Christian, ready for the "battle" at hand.

PRAYER:

Dear God, help me to be a good soldier of Christ. I want to obey you and be a loyal follower. Give me the courage to tell others about Jesus and His love for them. In Jesus' name, amen.

SADDLE UP! (What would God have you do now?)

Have you ever thought of yourself as a soldier? Write two things you can do to show others you are a good soldier of Jesus Christ:

_____

_____

Take your ride: (Do you know?)

The best way to recognize an Austrian Warmblood is by a brand, the letter "A," placed on the left hip of foals.

Dismount and cool down your horse! (Do you know?)

"Put on the whole armor of God, that ye may be able to stand against the wiles of the devil" (Ephesians 6:11).

Day 13

The Azerbaijan: A Burden Lifter

"Bear ye one another's burdens, and so fulfill the law of Christ."
(Galatians 6:2)

Have you ever heard of an Azerbaijan (AZ-ər-by-JAHN)? Not many people have. In fact, if you'd ask the average person, he might say he thinks an Azerbaijan is a type of insect or some disease!

The Azerbaijan horse, (once called a Kazakh), is as unknown as the country of Azerbaijan itself. This small republic lies just northwest of Iran in Eurasia. Although Azerbaijan is small, its people have great respect and pride for a powerful little horse that owes his roots to that part of the world. The little-known breed is a mountain-steppe racing and riding horse. These tough horses are known for living long lives and having great endurance. They do very well growing up in herds on mountainsides, and they're strong with lots of spunk.

If you'd like to look at a handsome horse, the Azerbaijan will fit the bill. He usually comes in the solid colors of chestnut, bay, or gray. He has a short head with a broad forehead and narrow nose, a really thick neck, and a strong body, and he runs fast with a pacing (a rather fast steady) gait. He runs so fast the Azerbaijan folks often hold races. This little equine powder keg has been clocked at almost a mile in about three minutes!

Azerbaijans are also known for strength and stamina, working as pack horses to lighten heavy loads for the people who love them so much. The breed has unique characteristics that have made him a reliable burden bearer. Although he's only about 11 to 12 hands, he can carry heavy loads on mountain trails and over the countryside with no problem. While carrying all that weight, he can go about 25 to 30 miles in one day!

Wow! The Azerbaijan certainly has the reputation of being a burden lifter. How about you? Do you help others and lift their burdens?

You might think, *How can I lift burdens and heavy things? I'm just a kid.*

Do you know the Bible teaches us to be burden lifters to our family and friends? Lifting burdens doesn't always mean picking up heavy things as you would do to help someone move into a new house or maybe just to clean out a garage. When you're a burden lifter, you can also be an encourager. You're someone who says kind words and does kind deeds to make others feel better. To do this, you should be alert to your family's and friends' needs.

If someone is disappointed about something, do you ever offer kind words? Do you listen if your friend wants to tell you his troubles? These are ways even children can be burden lifters like the perky Azerbaijan.

Perhaps you don't think about how others are feeling because you think about yourself too much. Or maybe you have too many of your own problems. The Bible tells us that we're to give our worries to the Lord Jesus, and He'll help us. When we pray, ask for His strength, and give our burdens to Him, He's ready to take them. God then gives us strength so we're ready and able to lift burdens for those we love.

PRAYER:

Dear God, help me to not focus on myself all the time. Help me to be sensitive to the burdens of others, so I can offer to help. In Jesus' name, amen.

SADDLE UP! (What would God have you do now?)

List some family or friends who have burdens. Write how you can offer to help:

_____

_____

_____

_____

_____

Take your ride: (Do you know?)

The Azerbaijan has a peculiar lengthwise fold on his tongue, making it look like a forked (divided) tongue.

Dismount and cool down your horse! (Do you know?)

"Come unto me, all ye that labour and are heavy laden, and I will give you rest" *(Matthew 11:28).*

Day 14

The Azteca: Full of Grace

*"For by grace are ye saved through faith;
and that not of yourselves: it is the gift of God:
Not of works, lest any man should boast."
(Ephesians 2:8-9)*

If you live in Mexico, you know what an Azteca (Azz-TECH-ah) horse is. Since the country of Mexico is only a little over 200 years old, you'd think the Azteca has been around for hundreds of years, as well. But this beautiful breed only appeared on the scene in 1972 when Mexican charros (cowboys) began to breed horses with great skill and lots of "cow sense" to work on their cattle ranches. The charros crossed Andalusians with their Quarter Horses and the little-known Criollo mares and got amazing results. This new breed, officially recognized by the Mexican Department of Agriculture in 1982, now had speed, strength, a sweet disposition with the desire to learn, and equine "grace." The Azteca became so popular, he's now known as The National Horse of Mexico.

You might think a horse with all these excellent traits would be a huge brute, but the Azteca only averages from 14.2 to 16 hands.

He can be any color or combination of colors accepted in the American Quarter Horse Association and the American Paint Horse Association. His head is a medium size with a broad forehead, alert eyes, and medium ears which are always twitching. His muscular neck arches slightly, and this little beauty often has a long flowing mane and just as spectacular a tail. Despite his average height, his free shoulders and hips allow him to be incredibly athletic and smooth to ride.

Whether you like English or western style riding or whether you need a graceful dancer or cow horse, the Azteca might be just for you. How about if you enjoy jumping, dressage, driving, cutting, penning, or reining? Or would you just love a wonderful companion for trail riding? Take a good look at the Azteca. He can do it all and do it well. All of these skills create a horse full of grace that anyone would be proud to own.

There's someone else who is full of grace too—the Lord Jesus Christ. In fact, He has more grace than anyone ever had or ever will have. He has so much grace, He willingly shares it with us!

Do you know what the word "grace" means? One of the definitions describes grace as having mercy or forgiveness, and that's exactly what Jesus did on the cross for us. He knew we could never be good enough to be allowed in heaven, so He died, rose from the dead, and is willing to save anyone by His grace. But there's another important meaning of the word grace.

Grace also means thoughtfulness toward others. If someone has grace in his life, he shows kindness and generosity toward his family and friends, even when he doesn't feel like it. As a Christian, when you show grace to others, your actions will show God how much you love Him and want to model your life after His. Then others might consider you as someone full of grace.

PRAYER:

Dear God, I'm thankful Jesus shed His blood so I can go to heaven someday. As hard as I try, I know I can never be good enough to be ready for heaven. Now I know what grace really means, and I want to give to others with your help. In Jesus' name, amen.

SADDLE UP! (What would God have you do now?)

List the names of a few people who have shown grace to you and explain how they did it.

_____

_____

_____

_____

_____

Take your ride: (Do you know?)

When Mexican breeders brought the Azteca to the United States, they crossbred him with American Paints to make a stunning, splashy horse called the American Azteca.

Dismount and cool down your horse! (Do you know?)

"But grow in grace, and in the knowledge of our Lord and Saviour Jesus Christ. To him be glory both now and for ever. Amen" (2 Peter 3: 18).

Day 15

The Barb: The Great Influencer

"They helped every one his neighbour;
and every one said to his brother,
Be of good courage."
(Isaiah 41:6)

The Barb, or Berber horse, is a hardy breed from northern African. It's a mystery where this horse developed, and it seems to be in competition with the Arabian as the oldest breed alive.

No one knows whether the Barb and Arabian horses share a common ancestor, or if the Arabian came before the Barb. Some believe the Barb originated in northern Africa during the 8th Century when Muslim invaders reached the region. Others believe the Barb's roots include the Arabian horse, the Akhal-Teke, and the Caspian horse. When imported to Europe, the Barbs were sometimes mistaken for Arabians, although they have very different physical traits. Regardless of the Barb's beginnings, the breed has a long history.

Standing only 14.2 to 15.2 hands, the Barb's a "light" riding horse noted for his stamina and fiery temperament combined with a gentle nature. Small stature doesn't stop this little guy from having a powerful front end, high withers (shoulders), short back, and a low tail. Although he isn't known for his gaits, he takes off quickly and gallops like a sprinter. The Barb thrives on meager rations, surefootedness, and speed over short distances. He also has perfect posture for carrying weight and loves to learn from his master. Because of these characteristics, beginning in the 16th Century, they were also trained for dressage in European capitals.

The Barb is now bred primarily in Morocco, Algeria, Spain, and southern France. Due to difficult economic times in North Africa, the number of purebred Barbs is decreasing. The World Organization of the Barb Horse, founded in Algeria in 1987, was formed to preserve the breed.

This spunky equine has had more of a profound effect on racing breeds throughout the world than any other horse except the Arabian. Berber invaders from North Africa took their Barbs to Europe from the early 8th Century on. Once established on the Iberian Peninsula (Spain and Portugal), the Barb bred with Spanish stock for 300 years to develop the Andalusian and the Lusitano.

You can notice the influence of the Barb in the Criollo from Argentina, the Paso Fino, and many other Western Hemisphere breeds including the Mustang and the Appaloosa. European noble families also valued the Barb, using the sturdy breed to establish large racing stables. Believe it or not, the Barb also found his way to the Bahamas as well.

Known as the Abaco Barb because it settled on Great Abaco Island in the Bahamas, this equine descended from horses that were shipwrecked during the Spanish colonization of the Americas and the Caribbean. The wild Barbs that ran free on Great Abaco once numbered over 200 horses. But this strain of the Barb breed was found in colors that were different from those of the European/African Barb, including pinto, roan, chestnut, black, and other colors. Unfortunately over the years, the horses died out and no longer roam the Bahamas.

Despite his declining numbers, the Barb, even though small in stature, may have been one of the most important horses in the start of numerous other breeds over the years, more than any other. What an influence this little horse has had on the equine world!

Speaking of influence, young people can have an influence on those around them. The word "influence" means to have the ability to affect others by the way we behave. Do you know you can have a good influence or a bad influence on others? Which would you like to be?

The Bible tells us that Christians are to have a positive influence on others. A positive influence means helping, encouraging, and giving. Do you willingly help your friends and family? Do you ever say a kind word to family members, or do you complain about the food on the table and the chores you're to do? And how about giving? If you get an allowance or earn money from your chores, do you give a tithe (10%) back to God?

If you feel God wants you to have more of a positive influence on others, pray and ask Him to help you. God will give you the desire and the ability to do so. Once you practice being a good influencer, you'll be happier than you've ever been before.

PRAYER:

Dear God, I want to be a positive influence on others. Help me to always be willing to help others and be ready to encourage and to give. In Jesus' name, amen.

SADDLE UP! (What would God have you do now?)

List a few ways you can be a good influencer and whom you'll influence.

_____

_____

_____

_____

_____

_____

_____

_____

Take your ride: (Do you know?)

An Abaco Barb stallion, Capella, was the model for a 2005 Breyer horse. That model became part of a publicity campaign to support the Barb's preservation.

Dismount and cool down your horse! (Do you know?)

"Be of good courage, and he shall strengthen your heart, all ye that hope in the LORD" (Psalm 31:24).

Day 16

The Belgian: A Determined Hard Worker

"Whether therefore ye eat, or drink, or whatsoever ye do,
do all to the glory of God."
(1 Corinthians 10:31)

Would you like to take a guess which country the Belgian Draft Horse came from?

If you said Belgium, you are absolutely correct.

It's believed Belgians may have originated as warhorses that carried knights with their heavy armor in the Middle Ages, although no evidence has proven that to be true. The Belgians are among the ancient breeds of Europe that contributed to the development of many other draft breeds. Whatever the case, their history goes back several hundred years.

After 1887, the breed found its way to America and became a very popular farm horse because of his size and strength. Until the 1940s, the Belgian and the Brabant, another big workhorse, were considered the same breed. But following World War II, the Brabant in Europe was bred to have a thicker, heavier body, while in the United States the Belgian breeders developed a somewhat taller horse with a lighter body. In fact, today the Belgian is the most numerous draft horse in the U.S.

The build of the Belgian shouts the word "power!" His head is square with either a straight or slightly concave profile. His short neck is muscular, and he has a wide back with a short body and deep girth. The strong legs are lean, allowing him to have a good gait. God made the Belgian perfect for lots of action and for draft work that uses every muscle in his gigantic frame.

The Belgian horse is considered by many horse enthusiasts to be the strongest and most powerful of all the draft horse breeds in the world. However, other equine lovers believe the Shire should hold that title. As of yet, no one has been able to make an "official" declaration because both breeds have very impressive statistics. So, the debate goes on.

But there's no debate about the awe and majesty of the Belgian breed. Talk about a big beauty! This horse stands between 16.2 and 17 hands. Then there's Big Jake, the tallest Belgian, born in 2000, that stands at 20.2 hands. On average, the Belgian grows to weigh slightly over 2,000 pounds. Yet, the heaviest Belgian, named Brooklyn Supreme, weighed 3,200 pounds and stood at 19.2 hands! You'd need a ladder to get on that big fella!

Most Belgians are a light chestnut, but they can be solid roan, bay, or black with a flaxen mane and tail and light to medium feathered (long, usually white hair) feet. Regardless of the color, they are a stunning presence when pulling a fancy wagon in a parade. But they're probably best known for their participation in draft competitions, mostly at fairs, where a team of two muscular Belgians pull with all their might to drag tremendous weights.

It's in the record books that at one of the National Western Stock Shows in Denver, Colorado, a team of two Belgians weighing only 4,800 pounds pulled 17,000 pounds a distance of 7 feet 2 inches. And at an Iowa State fair, the heavyweight champs in the pulling contest pulled 14,600 pounds a distance of 15 feet. The team consisted of one Belgian and one Percheron weighing just 3,600 pounds together.

Despite Belgians' amazing strength, they're also well known for their kindness and easy-going manner. In fact, they take the bit and bridle as easy as though eating a juicy apple. They seem to have one goal while working so hard. As determined as they are to win, they want to please even more.

How determined are you to work hard for the Lord Jesus? Do you strive to please Him in everything you do, or do you think you might have a lazy streak that tempts you to do the least amount of work you're asked to do?

God's Word has much to say about the way Christians should do their jobs, whether they are at home, at school, or helping others. The Bible says that everything we do, hard work or not, we're to do it first for the Lord then for our parents or others who've asked us to do something for them.

So, when you're asked to "pull a heavy load," that means to do a job you think you can't do (or don't want to do), remember the determined Belgian, and work as hard you can for God, no matter what you're asked to do. The Lord will be very pleased.

PRAYER:

Dear God, help me to be a determined hard worker. I want to please you in everything I do. In Jesus' name, amen.

SADDLE UP! (What would God have you do now?)

Maybe you think your homework or the little jobs you do around the house aren't very important. But any task you do *is* important if you do it for Him. List a few chores you're asked to do regularly. Write how you might be able to do those jobs better.

_____

_____

_____

_____

_____

Take your ride: (Do you know?)

The "dynamometer" is a machine created to test the greatest pulling power of horse teams in pulling competitions at fairs and horse shows.

Dismount and cool down your horse! (Do you know?)

"We work hard with our own hands…" (1 Corinthians 4:12a NIRV).

Day 17

The Brandenburger: Going for the Gold!

"…the judgments of the Lord are true and righteous altogether. More to be
desired are they than fine gold, yea, than much fine gold: sweeter also than
the honey and the honeycomb. Moreover by them is thy servant warned:
and in keeping of them there is great reward."
(Psalm 19: 9b-11)

The Brandenburger has his roots way back in the 15th Century in Brandenburg, a state in northeast Germany. This breed developed out of the need for a good work horse in agriculture. Farmers soon discovered this equine had no problem thriving in Germany's climate, whether facing hot summers or harsh winters. So for centuries, this strong horse served his owners mostly by plowing fields and pulling wagons.

In 1922, the Warmblood Breeding Society began to help align farming needs for the horse with proper breeding. Gradually, a stronger but gentle warmblood developed by crossing Hanoverian and Prussian breeds. Right after World War II, a stallion named

Komet from Mecklenburg, East Germany, miraculously escaped a horrible enforced castration rule for unapproved stallions in that country. He later sired a series of successful show jumping champions. Eventually, this breed gained a reputation as a fantastic sport horse during the mid-20th Century by crossbreeding Trakehners (TRACK en ners), Hanoveranians, English Thoroughbreds, Oldenburgs, and Holsteiners.

By 1999, 1,927 broodmares and 76 sires had been registered. Germany has long been recognized for its warmblood horse breeding. This horse is a testament to that long tradition of valuable warm-blooded German horses that shine as excellent sport horses as well as farm workers.

The typical Brandenburg is about 16.1 hands. He has a medium head, a well-set neck with a long and straight back, and muscled, strong legs. His common color is bay, usually with dark markings on the ankles and legs. Sometimes you might spot a white marking on his forehead, and his coat is often shiny, like a brand-new penny.

This snappy breed is a well-balanced horse with a lively temperament. Yet, he's easy going with the tendency to be nervous. He does well at dressage, endurance riding, general riding, and driving. As a warmblood, he's a combination of the speed and agility of the hotbloods and the heavier build and gentlemanly manners of the coldbloods.

So what do we have today with this gorgeous Brandenburger? Remember, he started out as a lowly farm animal, pulling plows and wagons. But his determination and drive to go for the gold made him a popular breed found in all spheres of riding and driving sports as well as in dressage and show jumping. His ultimate achievement has been his arrival on the Olympic scene, where he's won more than his share of gold medals.

How about you? Do you have goals in your life that might lead to "gold" someday? Do you know you can go for the gold right now at your age?

The Bible tells us that God's Word is more precious than gold, and if we spend time reading it, we'll gain wisdom and knowledge. A wise person makes decisions that bring success in his life. Who wouldn't want to be successful in any venture he'd try? According to the Bible, those who take special heed to God's "judgments," or his Word, will earn great rewards.

So, when you read your Bible, remember that the wisdom you're learning is more valuable than all the money in the world. You'll be on the road to success in whatever you strive to do. And you'll on your way to winning the gold!

PRAYER:

Dear God, I want to be the best at anything you ask me to do. Please give me the desire to please you. Help me to be in your Word every day so I can gain wisdom. In Jesus' name, amen.

SADDLE UP! (What would God have you do now?)

If you don't have a regular time to read your Bible every day, now might be the time to decide to do that, which will help you "go for the gold." Write when you think would be the best time for you to have your daily devotional time:

_____

_____

Take your ride: (Do you know?)

Poetin, a Brandenburger mare and blue-ribbon dressage horse, sold for a record amount at a PSI (Performance Sales International) auction in 2003 for three-and-a-half million dollars.

Dismount and cool down your horse! (Do you know?)

"But he knoweth the way that I take: when he hath tried me, I shall come forth as gold" (Job 23:10).

Day 18

The Camarillo: Not a Fake!

"I am not ashamed of the gospel, because it is the power of God for the salvation of everyone who believes: first for the Jew, then for the Gentile."
(Romans 1:16 NIRV)

Have you ever watched the Tournament of Roses Parade in Pasadena, California, on TV on New Year's Day? If so, then you've probably oohed and aahed at every horse marching down the street. One of the breeds featured has been the Camarillo. Do you know your horse breeds well enough to recognize a Camarillo?

Besides appearing in the Rose Parade, the Carmarillo has become famous, mostly in California, for their performances in all kinds of parades and events. They have such a reputation on the West Coast that several famous people have owned or ridden them, including former President Ronald Reagan.

But what's so unusual about the Camarillo?

Most horses classified as "white" are not true white. They're often born with a dark coat, which turns lighter with age and looks like it might be white, but the horses are really gray because of their dark skin.

However, the Camarillo is not a fake. He's known for his pure white color, which includes pink skin under his dazzling white coat. This amazing horse is white from birth and remains so his entire life.

The Camarillo is not only a color breed. He has other distinctive characteristics, including a refined body shape. He has beautiful large eyes, an arching neck, and strong legs.

Where did this head-turning beauty get his start?

Around 1912, a pure white Mustang colt with brown eyes came on the scene. As he frolicked in the pasture, no one ever thought he'd become the foundation stallion for the Camarillo White Horse. Over the next 95 years, he founded a new horse breed, carried the Camarillo name, and gained a reputation as an equine legend.

So, how did all this happen?

In 1921, Adolfo Camarillo bought a dazzling white stallion (yep, the little white colt born nine years ago) named "Sultan" at the California State Fair in Sacramento. Mr. Camarillo loved the horse so much, he called him "a stallion of a dream." He and Sultan worked as a team in many competitions and became well-known for all their victories throughout California.

Knowing he had a special white horse, Mr. Camarillo bred Sultan to Morgan mares at the Camarillo Ranch, developing a line owned only by the Camarillo family for the next 65 years. When Mr.

Camarillo died in 1958, his daughter Carmen continued breeding Camarillos. She also continued to show the horses at parades and events until her death in 1987, when, at her wish, the horses were sold at public auction, ending the exclusive ownership of the breed by the Camarillo family.

In 1989, five Camarillo lovers decided to regroup the horses for public performances. But by 1991, only eleven horses remained, and the breed was in danger of dying out. Thus, the Camarillo White Horse Association began the following year.

Today, several owners continue to breed and parade the Camarillo White Horses to maintain the lineage and keep the story of the special white horse alive. (As of 2010 there were only 20 known Camarillos: three stallions, five mares, three geldings, two two-year-old colts and seven foals.)

The Camarillo White Horse has become part of an international study to determine what genes are responsible for making a truly white horse. With several populations of white horses as part of the study, it was discovered that the Camarillo White Horse carries a unique mutation of a certain gene partially responsible for the coat color found only in that breed. It can now be determined if a white horse that someone believes may be a Camarillo White Horse is truly such, or whether he's a fake.

Exactly what is a fake? A fake is someone who tries to make something seem real that isn't. A fake deceives others.

Did anyone ever think you are a fake?

If I asked your friends if they think you're a Christian, what would they say? Would they say, "I don't think he's a Christian. He's never said he is. Sometimes he doesn't act like it either."

If you're a believer in Jesus, are you faking it? Are you pretending you're not a Christian when you're with your friends because you're ashamed of God? Maybe you'd like to be a brave witness for the Lord Jesus Christ, but sometimes you're not sure what to say.

The best thing to do is pray and ask God for the right words. As you read your Bible and go to church regularly, you'll learn how to share the gospel with your friends. As you do that, they'll soon respect you for your beliefs and will never consider you a fake at all.

PRAYER:

Dear God, help me not to be a "fake" in front of my friends. I always want to be honest and be brave enough to tell them I'm a Christian and that Jesus is the Savior. In Jesus' name, amen.

SADDLE UP!   (What would God have you do now?)

Are there any of your friends who don't know you're a Christian because you've not been honest with them? List their names here, and ask God to give you the courage to stand up for your faith in Christ.

_____

_____

_____

Take your ride: (Do you know?)

The Camarillo White Horse is the official horse of the city of Camarillo, California.

Dismount and cool down your horse! (Do you know?)

"Providing for honest things, not only in the sight of the Lord, but also in the sight of men" (2 Corinthians 8:21).

Day 19

The Canadian Horse: "Little Iron Horse"

"Let them give thanks to the Lord for his unfailing love and his wonderful deeds for men, for he breaks down gates of bronze and cut through bars of iron."
(Psalm 107: 15-16 NIRV)

In the late 1600s, King Louis XIV of France sent two different breeds of horses, the Breton and Norman, to a region we now call Quebec, Canada. Those two breeds are believed to be the ancestors of the modern Canadian Horse. Today the Canadian Horse possesses traits similar to the Arabian, Andalusian, and Barb that the Breton and Norman horses had so very long ago—rugged, strong, dashing, and quick.

The Breton and Norman multiplied with little interference for hundreds of years, resulting in a beautiful yet tough little equine, the Canadian Horse or Cheval Canadien. The limited number of those first horses in the newly-founded Canadian colony meant they were highly valued, and since they were so isolated from the rest of the known world, the breed remained pure. Thus, the horse became a versatile helper to the new colonists even through harsh weather and sparse food supplies. His jobs included farm work, driving stagecoaches, riding, and racing. Because this equine trooper excelled at any task he was asked to do, he earned the nickname "Little Iron Horse."

Because the Canadian Horse had such strong traits, in the mid-1800s he became popular in the United States as well as in Canada where he was crossbred to improve the strength of other breeds. The Morgan, Tennessee Walking Horse, Standardbred, and American Saddlebred can all thank the Canadian Horse for their stamina and determination.

Soon the Canadian Horses earned such a reputation, many were exported to southern Africa to work on sugar plantations in the West Indies and to pull wagons and cannons in the U.S. Civil War where many were killed. With so many horses leaving Canada, the war, and the invention of farm machines and automobiles, the Canadian Horse nearly became extinct.

But that's when Canadian Horse lovers saved the breed in 1886, starting the first studbook. Nine years later the Canadian Horse Breeders Association was formed to further preserve the horse. However, today the breed is still listed as critical by the American Livestock Conservancy with only an estimated 2,000 Canadian Horses on record. Yet, the future of the breed is looking brighter as horse lovers in Canada work endlessly to preserve this special horse.

The Canadian Horse stands 14 to 16 hands, weighs 900-1000 pounds, and is usually black or bay with a long flowing mane and tail. He has lots of well-developed muscles and has a handsome arched neck. This overachiever is energetic without being nervous and has great strength to fulfill the tasks asked of him. Is it any wonder he's called the "Little Iron Horse?"

The word "iron" always indicates strength and power. Do you know there are verses in the Bible that tell us that God is so powerful, He can bend iron? Our Wonderful Lord has the strength and might to do anything He wants. He's so strong and mighty, He created the universe and the heavens in just six days. If we worship a God who is so powerful, don't you think He's able to help us with our troubles?

God can, and will, help us. All we need to do is ask. The next time you have a problem that seems to overwhelm you, take it to the Lord in prayer. If God can bend iron, He certainly can give you the wisdom and strength you need.

PRAYER:

Dear God, thank you for being such a strong God, strong enough to cut through bars of iron. I know I can depend on you for my strength to solve problems in my life. In Jesus' name, amen.

SADDLE UP! (What would God have you do now?)

Think about how God displays his power and strength in your life or in the world around you. Write some of the things you've observed.

_____

_____

_____

_____

_____

Take your ride: (Do you know?)

A few chestnut-colored Canadian Horses have been found occasionally with flaxen manes and tails, and the cream gene appears rarely as the result of interbreeding with just one cream-colored stallion.

Dismount and cool down your horse! (Do you know?)

"Iron he treats like straw and bronze like rotten wood" (Job 41:27 NIRV).

Day 20

The Caspian: Runs the Race to Win!

*"Know ye not that they which run in a race run all,
but one receiveth the prize? So run, that ye may obtain."
(1 Corinthians 9:24)*

If you like Arabians, you'll probably like Caspians. Caspians have the beauty and endurance of the Arabian and the build of a miniature Thoroughbred.

The Caspian originated in northern Iran. Horse enthusiasts believe this breed is one of the most ancient equines, possibly going back over 4000 years. Archaeological remains found in northern Iran of a little horse with a light frame, refined head with large eyes, short ears, and small muzzle seem to support that theory. Even though his height ranges only between nine and 11.2 hands, he's classified a horse rather than a pony because of his body shape, different gaits, and gentle nature.

So, how did the equine world first learn of this fantastic little horse?

For many years, Caspians were thought to have been extinct. But in 1965, Louise Firouz, a horse-loving American known as "the Lady of Horses," discovered a small horse in the Elborz Mountains of northern Iran while searching for ponies for American children. She thought she had found a chestnut bay pony pulling a cart. However, on closer inspection, she realized the stallion had the body of a horse. She purchased him, positive he had Caspian blood. When blood and DNA samples were tested, sure enough, archeo-zoologists proved the breed had come from a miniature Mesopotamian horse. These horses had managed to survive in small numbers because they lived between a mountain chain and the Caspian Sea with no outside influence.

Louise kept her spunky two-year-old stallion at her farm near Teheran for a year and trained him to take a rider and to drive different carts. She then brought him to America on a long flight, including five different layovers and six days of quarantine in New York. Though all of that ordeal, the little horse remained calm yet curious, both strong traits of Caspians.

He finally arrived at his new home in Virginia where he spent the rest of his life participating in exhibitions and shows. Although there were no Caspian mares in the U.S., he sired quite a few part-bred foals before his death in 1993.

Fortunately, the Caspian breed did not disappear from the scenes at that time. Caspian horse lovers determined to increase the breed's numbers and status in the equine world. From 1994 until the present, dozens of Caspian studs and mares came to America, thus increasing horse enthusiasts' knowledge of the rare breed.

In 2008, the Caspians still numbered only about 1600. At last count, the U.S. claims to have over 500 of the special horses. The good news is they're no longer in danger of becoming extinct. That shouldn't happen with horse lovers like the Caspian Horse Society of the Americas Official Registry and Mrs. Firouz's children, who work endlessly to preserve the breed.

If you want to find Caspians, you'll have to attend horse shows where you might find this little equine in different events. One of his favorites is scurry driving, where he races his little heart out to win. In fast-paced Double Harness Scurry Driving, two ponies, or horses like the Caspians, pull a carriage around a course of cones in fast time without knocking down the cones. Competitions take place in the U.S., Australia, New Zealand, and northern Europe, including England.

If you're not sure you're looking at a Caspian, remember the difference between him and a pony. The Caspian's coat is shiny and solid, including solid gray tones that might look white, and he has a deep girth with well-developed hindquarters. If you're close enough to see his hooves, they're oval-shaped and are rarely shod, even under extreme conditions. But one thing is certain about the Caspian. He runs every race with one goal in mind: to cross the finish line first.

Do you run races with the passion like the little Caspian does?

I'm not only talking about races you might run with your friends during field days or just fun in the backyard.

The Bible tells us that as Christians, we're to serve God as though we're running a race. That means we should strive to please Him to the best of our ability. The Bible tells us we will earn rewards, or "prizes," like gorgeous crowns in heaven if we serve God faithfully now and do it with smiles on our faces.

Do you get up every morning with the determination to please the Lord? If you do, then you are "running your race to win!"

PRAYER:

Dear God, I want to "run a strong race" for you in everything I do. Please give me the desire and courage so I don't quit when things get hard. In Jesus' name, amen.

SADDLE UP! (What would God have you do now?)

Can you list what God might have you do to "run the race" better? Could it be obeying at home? Spending more time reading your Bible? Just being thankful more instead of complaining?

_____

_____

_____

Take your ride: (Do you know?)

The Caspian is different from all other breeds in a really strange way. He has an extra molar in his upper jaw.

Dismount and cool down your horse! (Do you know?)

"Therefore we also, since we are surrounded by so great a cloud of witnesses, let us lay aside every weight, and the sin which so easily ensnares us, and let us run with endurance the race that is set before us. Looking unto Jesus, the author and finisher of our faith …" (Hebrews 12:1-2a NKJV).

Day 21

The Chincoteague Pony: Redeemed!

"For I know that my redeemer liveth, and that he shall stand
at the latter day upon the earth."
(Job 19: 25)

Every year, as many as 50,000 horse lovers from all over the world gather the last Wednesday and Thursday of July to watch "Saltwater Cowboys" swim a pony herd from Assateague Island to Chincoteague Island on the Maryland/Virginia border. The Chincoteague Volunteer Fire Company in Virginia owns and manages the herd of about 300, with 150 adult ponies making the five-to-ten-minute swim. Both the cowboys and the observers are on hand to assist horses, especially foals, which may have a hard time crossing.

Wild ponies have lived on Assateague Island for hundreds of years. Some believe these special equines can trace their origin to early settlers releasing the horses to forage on the island. However, most people believe the ponies are the descendants of the survivors of a Spanish galleon that wrecked off the coast of Assateague hundreds of years ago. The large number of shipwrecks on record along with the fact that it was common for ships to transport ponies to the colonies of South America make it likely that the ponies originally got to Assateague from a shipwreck.

Because the Assateague Island is a harsh environment for any animal, the ponies' diet is limited, so they've had to adapt. Quite unusual is their main food of saltwater-saturated cord grass in the marshes on Assateague Island. They eat almost all day long just to get enough nutrition to sustain themselves.

The wild ponies congregate in small groups called "bands." (We usually call large groups of horses "herds.") Each band has one dominant stallion with a nice group of mares that have foals by him. About 70 foals are born every spring on the Virginia side of Assateague Island. Also, an average of 75 percent of the adult mares have foals every year, a high foaling rate for wild horses.

In 1994 to make sure the special ponies would be recognized, the Chincoteague Pony became an official registered breed. His average height is between 12 and 13 hands (Any "horse" that stands less than 14 hands is considered a pony). He's stocky with short legs, thick mane, and a large, round belly. You'll find Chincoteagues in any solid colors, but most of them are pinto.

A very interesting fact about the sale of Chincoteague Ponies concerns the preservation of the breed. Just so the ponies don't dwindle into extinction, a few select foals in excellent shape are designated as "buybacks" at the annual sale. A buyback pony is auctioned with the stipulation that the person who buys the pony will donate him back to the fire company and return him to Assateague Island to help replenish the herd. The winner of a buyback pony gets a certificate from the fire company and gets to name the pony before it's returned to Assateague Island.

Buyback or "redeemed" ponies are very popular and have actually become some of the highest priced foals sold at the auction. As of 2015, the highest price paid for a pony was $25,000 and the lowest price was $500. If you ever go to the Chincoteague Pony roundup, do you think you'd like to bid on a pony to redeem it?

Do you know if you're a Christian, you've also been redeemed? The words "redeemed" and "redeemer" are mentioned in over 120 verses in the Bible. They tell us that Jesus created us. In other words, He "owned" us, but our sin separated us from Him. We were "lost." But because Jesus loves us so much, He came to earth to die on the cross so we could have our sins forgiven. That's how He redeemed us. We became "buybacks." The Bible tells us Jesus became our Redeemer so those who believe in Him can go to heaven someday.

If you've asked Jesus to be your Savior, then you've been redeemed!

PRAYER:

Dear God, thank you for being my Savior and Redeemer. Thank you for "buying me back" when you died on the cross for my sins. In Jesus' name, amen.

SADDLE UP!   (What would God have you do now?)

Can you explain what "redeem" means to your friends by using this example: "My dog that I just bought at the pet store was lost for over a month. But then ….

_____

_____

_____

_____

_____

Take your ride: (Do you know?)

To compensate for all the salt in the cord grass the ponies eat, they drink twice as much water as a normal horse. That's why their bellies always look bloated.

Dismount and cool down your horse! (Do you know?)

"But when the fullness of the time had come, God sent forth His Son, born of a woman, born under the law, might receive the adoption as sons" (Galatians 4:4-5).

Pepsi

Day 22

The Cleveland Bay:
Welcomed at the Royal Palace

*"The Spirit Himself bears witness with our spirit that we are children of
God, and if children, then heirs—heirs of God and joint heirs with Christ."
(Romans 8:16-17a)*

If a horse is named a "bay," can you guess what color he is?
Right! He's a shade of brown with a black mane, black tail, and black
stockings. He could be a golden chestnut or as dark as milk
chocolate, but he'd still have those black trimmings. And that's
exactly what we've got with the Cleveland Bay!

The Cleveland Bay is the oldest breed from England, believed
to date back to the 17th Century. He's named after his consistent bay
colors and the Cleveland district in Yorkshire. Although this horse is
always labeled "bay," a few light hairs are sometimes found in the
mane and tail of some. Breeders prefer bays with a more reddish tint
than other shades. However, if any white markings appear on a colt,

except for a small star on the forehead, he's not able to be registered in the stud book. The shades of bay are important when creating matching driving pairs because drivers want their teams to look almost identical.

The earliest breeding of the Bay was done mostly by church members and priests in monasteries in the Middle Ages. They needed pack horses to carry trade goods between abbeys and monasteries in northeast England. Those pack horses were eventually crossbred with Andalusians and Barbs and later with Arabians and Thoroughbreds to create the lighter-in-weight Cleveland Bay of today.

Over the next few hundred years, interest in the Bay waned, mostly because of the invention of the automobile. In the early and mid-20th Century, breeders started using Bays as hunters. Unfortunately, breeders soon lost interest in them, and by 1962, only four stallions were left in England. But then Queen Elizabeth II, knowing the breed was used to drive royal carriages since the1920s, took a personal interest in the Bay and saved it by purchasing Mulgrave Supreme, a stallion that was about to be sold to a U.S. buyer. The queen and Prince Philip, Duke of Edinburg, did all they could to preserve the breed, and within 15 years there were 36 purebred stallions in the United Kingdom. Because the prince used the breed in international driving competitions in the late 1960s and 1970s, horse lovers became more interested then wanted part-bred Cleveland Bays for riding horses, hunters, and jumpers. In 1964, a

Cleveland Bay/ Thoroughbred even competed in show jumping in the Tokyo Olympics!

Since 1977, Elizabeth II has been a patron of the British Cleveland Bay Horse Society and has worked tirelessly to preserve this special horse. Yet, despite her efforts, the UK Rare Breeds Survival Trust considers the Bay's numbers to be critical with less than 300 mares registered. At last count, it's been reported only about 550 Cleveland Bays exist worldwide.

Cleveland Bays have a sweet, calm temperament and stand between 16 and 16.2 hands. They have a muscular body and strong legs that seem a little too short for the stout body. They're versatile, performing well at driving, show jumping, and farm work. But best of all, Bays have been fortunate enough to be chosen by the British Royal Family for almost a century and are still used to pull carriages in royal processions today.

As you think about the Cleveland Bay being part of the Queen's royal palace, do you realize if you've asked Jesus Christ to be your Savior, you're included in the royal family of the God of the Universe? The Bible says if we've accepted Jesus, God has adopted us into His royal eternal family, and we are heirs of His kingdom. Every Christian is considered a child of the King. The Bible also tells us we are sons of God, and one day we'll inherit all that God has, including beautiful homes in heaven.

Of course, you're already part of your human family here on earth whether you're naturally born into that family or adopted. Your family members love you and have given you all the rights and privileges available as part of that family. How cool is that?

Since you're a member of your human family, do you represent the family well? Do you act responsibly as a young Christian? Perhaps a parent has said this: "Act like you're part of our family. Make me proud of you."

Do you know God our Heavenly Father also wants His children to make Him proud?

As a member of God's family, do you try to please Him and make Him proud? Maybe you never realized you are a child of the King. If you face every new day with the desire to obey not only your parents but God as well, then you'll make all of them proud.

PRAYER:

Dear God, I realize you are my heavenly Father, and I'm your child. I pray I can live every day to please you. Please help me do that. In Jesus' name, amen.

SADDLE UP! (What would God have you do now?)

List some things you can do to make God and your family proud.

_____

_____

_____

_____

_____

Take your ride: (Do you know?)

Today Cleveland Bays make up the majority of the bay horses in the Royal Mews, the British royal stables, where they receive intense training to pull royal carriages.

Dismount and cool down your horse! (Do you know?)

"For ye are all the children of God by faith in Christ Jesus"
(Galatians 3:26).

Day 23

The Clydesdale: One Powerful Equine!

"Finally, my brethren, be strong in the Lord and in the power of his might."
(Ephesians 6:10)

The Clydesdale is a huge, coldblooded draft horse that has his roots as a farm animal from the Clyde Valley in Scotland, a country in Europe. He's considered a member of an exclusive equine club, "The Big Four of the Draft World," with Belgians, Percherons, and Shires. It might be well to note that the Clydesdale is as beautiful as he is big.

Way back in the 1700s, the breed developed from Flemish (northern Belgium) stallions that had been imported to Scotland and crossbred with local mares. The name "Clydesdale" was first used in 1826, and by 1830 a system of hiring stallions resulted in Clydesdale horses becoming popular throughout Scotland and northern England. In 1877, Clydesdale enthusiasts started the first breed registry, which raised great interest in the horse.

In the late 19th and early 20th Centuries, thousands of Clydesdales found their way from Scotland to the rest of the horse world, including Australia and New Zealand, where they were given the name "the breed that built Australia." However, during World War I, as with most horse breeds, Clydesdales began to decline due to automobiles and the invention of farm machinery. Unfortunately, the decline continued until 1970, when the Rare Breeds Survival Trust then declared the Clydesdale in danger of extinction. Clydesdale enthusiasts began to work to preserve the breed, and because of their efforts this majestic equine started to make a comeback.

So how big is big? Clydesdales stand from 16 to 18 hands and weigh 1,800 to 2,000 pounds. Now that's big. Some full-grown males have measured18 hands and weigh up to 2,200 pounds. That's almost as heavy as a small car! Despite the horses' size, would you believe some people actually like to ride them? You'd definitely need a ladder to get on, like climbing on the top of bunkbeds. And I imagine it would be like trying to ride a sofa!

Concerning the Clydesdales' colors, they're considered the dark horses of the Big Four. They're mostly bay, brown, roan, or black with white markings, mostly on the face and sometimes with large white blotches on his underbelly. They also have white feathers preferably on all four feet. Feathers? If you're a horse lover, then you probably already know that horses don't have "feathers" like birds do. You'd also know when a horse has feathers, he has long, flowing hair covering his feet.

The Clydesdale is quite the unique horse. Despite his bulky size and bulging muscles, he has a gorgeous arching neck and a flashy, high-step. He has lots of energy, and even when he pulls an oversized wagon or a heavy load, his power and beauty leave the admirer in awe. Besides his handsome frame, his mane will probably be braided and his tail either bobbed or braided, which only adds to his stunning appearance.

Some of the most famous members of the breed are the teams that make up the eight-horse hitches of the Budweiser Clydesdales. Also, Clydesdales and Shires are used by the British Household Cavalry as drum horses, leading parades during state occasions. Drum horses, of course, carry drums, and have the special privilege of guarding the Sovereign and the Royal Household. To qualify for that job, a drum horse must stand at least 17 hands because he'll carry the Musical Ride Officer and two silver drums, each weighing about 125 pounds. Only a powerful horse like the Clydesdale could handle all that weight and still prance with an arched neck.

Just as the Clydesdale uses his power to pull heavy loads and serve people, do you know you can ask God for His power to help you serve others too?

Perhaps you have situations in your life that make you feel weak and unable to know what to do. We all have problems in our lives that sometimes can stump us and cause us to want to "run away" from the trouble. But God is always with us, ready to help.

As a Christian, remember that your power to do right and to accomplish anything comes from God. Jesus is your best friend. All you need to do is ask Him, and you'll receive the power and strength to get the job done or solve the problem.

PRAYER:

Dear God, sometimes I feel very weak in my faith. I know I can be stronger with your power. Help me to always trust in you with important decisions. In Jesus' name, amen.

SADDLE UP! (What would God have you do now?)

List some things you think God will help you do to become a stronger Christian.

_____

_____

_____

_____

_____

Take your ride: (Do you know?)

In past days, the Clydesdales' feet were so big they couldn't fit in the farmers' plowed furrows. Thus, Clydesdales often worked in towns pulling wagons rather than pulling plows on farms.

Dismount and cool down your horse! (Do you know?)

"He gives power to the weak, and to those who have no might He increases strength" (Isaiah 40:29).

Day 24

The Curly Horse:
The Odd Ball of the Horse World

"But you are a chosen generation ... a peculiar people; that ye should shew forth the praises of him who hath called you out of darkness into his marvellous light."
(1 Peter 2:9)

Curlies come in all sizes and colors, but what's really strange about these horses is they all carry a gene for a uniquely curly coat of hair. Just as strange is how the breed originated.

In the early 20th Century, rancher John Damele and his sons near Eureka, Nevada, spotted a herd of Mustangs with a few strange-looking horses. While Mustangs were a common sight, the curly-coated horses were unusual. Years later, the Dameles managed to catch one. They trained it and rode it, then sold it, thus starting their Curly association. In 1932, a harsh winter hit, and when spring brought warmer weather, the only horses found were the Curlies.

The Dameles noted how hardy those few horses were, so they decided to include more of them in their herd.

After another harsh winter in 1952, the Dameles became serious about breeding the Curlies. They found the Mustangs again and rounded up a two-year-old chestnut stallion. Because the Dameles didn't care to keep the Curly breed pure and just wanted to improve their own horses, they crossbred their herd with one Morgan and one Arabian stallion. Those two studs and the Curly created beautiful foals with Curly blood. Thus, we have hundreds of cross-bred Curlies today. They can be found in gaited, sport, draft, pony, and even in a few miniature horses.

How the Curlies ever came to America in the first place remains a big question. Some historians surmise the horses were brought by Spanish Conquistadors, Russians, or Vikings. Early American Sioux natives regarded Curlies as sacred mounts for their chiefs and medicine men. Native American artwork also shows warriors riding this odd breed in the Battle of Little Bighorn.

If you want a horse for just a "cute pet," the Curly might be for you. You might say he looks like an overgrown poodle! At birth he has tight curls everywhere, even in his ears. As he matures, his coat settles down a little. His winter coat is still really tight, but in the summer his coat is wavy. However, some purebred Curlies have no curls at all and are called "smooth coats." And there's great news for you who are allergic to animal hair. You could actually own a Curly because the breed is hypo-allergenic. Curlies' hair doesn't trigger allergies!

As odd as the Curlies are, it seems they all have positive traits, perfect for children. Curlies have friendly manners and are easy to train despite their rugged determination. Most of them work hard, including participating in gymkhana (horse and rider events with speed/pattern racing and timed games).

Curlies come in nearly all colors and coat patterns, and the height varies according to type. Their colors are mostly chestnut but can be bay, black, or gray with appaloosa or pinto markings. Because of their crossbreeding with gaited horses, some Curlies have a running walk. Those saddle types range from 14.1 to 15.1 hands. Most other Curlies stand between 14 and 16 hands, but they can range from miniature horses to draft horses.

You're probably wondering how you groom a Curly. Remember, his curls can be as tight as a poodle's. Caring for the coat requires simple brushing. However, the mane is often not combed because the hair tends to lose its curl. Because the manes tangle easily, they're often trimmed real short.

By now, you probably agree the Curly Horse is an odd but beautiful horse. Another word for odd is the word "peculiar."

Many people consider Christians odd or peculiar. Are you a peculiar Christian?

The Bible tells us that Christians are peculiar in that we are special members of God's family. When we give our lives to Jesus, we have different ways of looking at things. We have different interests than those who aren't Christians.

Does everyone you know love to go to church and read the Bible, two activities Christians should want to do? Think about some friends who might not be Christians. What are they interested in? Because you choose not to do some of those things, those friends might actually call you "odd."

If others think you're odd, that's no reason to be sad. God calls you a *good* kind of peculiar because you do love Him and want to please Him. For that, you can be very thankful.

PRAYER:

Dear God, sometimes it's hard to be so different from some my friends. I want to be a strong Christian, even if others think I'm an oddball. Please help me to be like the Curly and not be ashamed of who I am and who You are. In Jesus' name, amen.

SADDLE UP!   (What would God have you do now?)

List some things you should do as a Christian that some of your friends might think is "odd." Ask God to help you be a good testimony.

_____

_____

_____

_____

_____

Take your ride: (Do you know?)

Some Curly owners collect their horses' shed hair from the manes and tails and donate it to the International Curly Horse Organization Fiber Guild. The guild uses the hair for making clothing. The proceeds go to ICHO Curly research efforts.

Dismount and cool down your horse! (Do you know?)

"Who gave himself for us, that he might redeem us from all iniquity, and purify unto himself a peculiar people, zealous of good works" (Titus 2:14).

Day 25

The Furioso-North Star: Fearless!

"There is no fear in love; but perfect love casteth out fear."
(1 John 4:18a)

The Furioso-North Star is a warm-blooded breed named after two stallions that started the line over 200 years ago. There's ongoing discussion whether the breed originated in Hungary or Romania, countries in Europe. Unfortunately, today The Furioso-North Star is endangered with only small numbers in those two countries and Slovakia. Those countries, involved in raising this rare horse for centuries, still have small herds grazing on their grasslands today. Because a few of these horses are only privately owned, the Furioso-North Star is considered a very valuable breed.

So, where did this horse get his start?

A beautiful English Thoroughbred named Furioso was foaled in 1836 at a stud farm in Hungary. Four years later, he was crossbred with Hungarian mares, which started the line of Furiosos. At about the same time, another Thoroughbred stallion, North Star, came from England and crossed with Hungarian mares. Those foals became known as the Furioso-North Star driving horses. North Star also sired foals of Norfolk Trotters and with Hungarian Nonius mares. By the end of the 19th Century, the two lines merged and were called Furioso-North Stars. North Stars produced great harness racehorses, and Furiosos produced excellent heavyweight riding horses.

The Furioso-North Star makes a noble appearance with a strong body. He has the reputation of having a calm temperament and learns quickly. He's a medium-heavy horse with a large frame that stands at 15.2 to 16.3 hands. He's mostly bay but can be chestnut or black. He's done light farm work, has performed in competition, and has been used in harness.

The Furioso is known as a good quality riding horse especially for one type of rider, the Csikos (CHI-kosh) from Hungary. They would say the Furioso faces any rider's challenge with a good attitude. The Furioso's shoulders and legs are muscular and strong enough to hold tremendous weights, even off-balanced ones like the trick-riding Csikos. And the horse does it with no fear!

Why would a horse fear any rider or anything the rider would do? We're not just talking about any rider.

The Csikos, mounted horse-herdsmen of Hungary, famous all over the world for their trick riding skills, often use the Furioso for their performances. What's unusual is how highly trained their horses are.

If you know anything about horses, then you know how "skittish" or overcautious most foals are. Many are afraid of loud noises, water in hoses, fire, or any fast movement around their bodies. Even as they mature, horses can fear the saddle or any weight on their backs as well as the bit in their mouth. We'll have to admit they're often big scaredy cats!

However, when trained properly from little up, especially for Csikos trick riders, Furiosos have no fear of anything the riders do. Some riders stand on their heads on the back of the horse, hang off the side of the horse, crawl under the horse's belly and come up the other side, carry flaming torches, or stand backwards on the saddle, and all of the tricks are done while the horse is galloping around an arena! The Furioso-North Stars are truly fearless!

Can you say you're fearless like the Furioso-North Star, or are you afraid of things? How about the dark? Spiders? Snakes? The bully in your school or neighborhood? Were you bitten by a dog once and now you're afraid of all dogs?

Most people have some fears about all kinds of things, and they might say it's just part of being human. However, do you know the Bible talks a lot about how we should handle our fears? God wants us to give all our fears and concerns to Him.

You might wonder how to do that. The Bible says to pray and ask God to give you courage then trust in the Lord for peace in your heart that only He can give. If you ask God to take the fears from you, He will. That doesn't mean the dangers are gone, but you'll be able to face them with a different attitude. God loves you, and love always takes away fears. With God on your side, you can conquer any fear you face.

PRAYER:

Dear God, I know You love me, and I can trust in You to take my fears away. Please help me to always remember that. In Jesus' name, amen.

SADDLE UP! (What would God have you do now?)

List some of your fears and ask God to take the fear from you. It might be a good time to discuss your fears with a parent.

_____

_____

_____

_____

_____

Take your ride: (Do you know?)

In 1784, the Hungarian Emperor Josef II founded the stud farm, Mezohegyes, which became one of Europe's great horse breeding centers.

Dismount and cool down your horse! (Do you know?)

"The Lord is my light and my salvation; whom shall I fear? The Lord is the strength of my life; of whom shall I be afraid?" (Psalm 27:1)

Ginger

Day 26

The Dutch Harness Horse: A High Stepper

"The steps of a good man are ordered by the Lord: and he delighteth in his way."
(Psalm 37:23)

For many centuries the Dutch (people from the Netherlands in Europe) concentrated on breeding high-stepping horses. Although farmers valued the horse as a helper and a source of income, they also considered a fancy horse a status symbol. And "fancy" is what we have with the Dutch Harness Horse.

The Dutch have a strong tradition of breeding driving horses. You might wonder what the difference is between a harness horse and a driving horse. There is no difference. The term "in harness" often describes a horse being driven. A horse harness is a type of tack with a breast collar that allows a horse to pull heavy vehicles such as carriages, wagons, or sleighs. The Dutch Harness Horse is noted for pulling lighter, fancier carriages in international competition. But where did he get his start?

During the late 19th and early 20th Centuries, the warm-blooded Dutch Harness Horses were known as "luxury horses." The first studbook in The Netherlands was founded in 1879, which started classifying them as a recognizable breed. It eventually emerged from two separate equines in the Netherlands. One breed, the northern Groningen, was heavier and had dark coats. The Gelderlander from southern Netherlands was taller and leggier and chestnut in color. Although the resulting horses were stout and could work on farms, they were also elegant with a high step to pull fancy carriages. Owners continued to improve their horses by breeding the best mares to the best trotting stallions. The result? The more streamlined and fancier "Sunday horses" became a separate line from the stronger working horses.

Because of those horses' classy development, their owners started competing to see whose equine was the showiest. When machines made farm horses unnecessary, the higher-steppers were bred for driving competition. Thus, by 1969, the Dutch Harness Horse became so popular, The Royal Warmblood Horse Studbook of the Netherlands (KWPN) was founded to preserve the breed.

As recent as the late 20th Century, more crossbreeding with Hackneys and Standardbreds resulted in a harness horse with stunning beauty and a natural high step. Today, although only 40 sires and fewer than 2,000 broodmares are registered, the Dutch Harness Horses are very easy to spot. In the past few years, a few have come to North America and have been crossbred with Arabians, where they are used as sport horses and saddle seat horses. Regardless of how they're shown, their fancy trot separates them from most other breeds. And there's a reason why.

The Dutch Harness Horse is unique in that he has strict rules when showing, and it has to do with his feet. The shoes must be within a certain width and thickness, and pads added to the hoof are prohibited. He's then able to step "to the high heavens" on his own, not because of special shoeing.

Besides his high stepping, the Dutch Harness Horse would have a braided mane and a natural tail in competition. He'd be decked with gorgeous tack, often wearing a white bridle with a cavesson (a noseband) that might match a white carriage. His coat colors can be chestnut, bay, brown, or black. However, he might be gray, a shade of roan, or a creme color. A tobiano paint Dutch Harness Horse surfaces occasionally, but he'd be rare. Regardless of the appearance of this beautiful horse, one fact is certain. He's proud to be high stepping for the one controlling his reins.

As the steps of a Dutch Harness Horse are in the hands of his driver, so are our steps in the hands of our Driver. Have you ever thought about your life and how each and every detail is planned by our Amazing God?

The Bible tells us that God has a plan for every Christian, and the Lord directs every step in the life of a believer who trusts in God's wisdom.

Do you pray and ask God for wisdom and for Him to direct your steps? If you have, then God directs your steps through those older and wiser such as a parent, a pastor, or a teacher. Obeying those people will make you a "high-stepper," allowing the Lord to direct your steps throughout your entire life.

PRAYER:

Dear God, I trust you with my life, and I want you to plan my steps. I'm willing to serve you in whatever you ask me to do. In Jesus' name, amen.

SADDLE UP!   (What would God have you do now?)

List what you think might be some "good" steps a young Christian should take in his life. Be determined to take those steps in your Christian walk with Jesus.

_____

_____

_____

_____

_____

Take your ride: (Do you know?)

Branding horses is now illegal in the Netherlands, so the red-lion-standing-on-his-hind-legs brand of the KWPN is found on the left thigh of only older horses. Today, KWPN horses are microchipped instead.

Dismount and cool down your horse! (Do you know?)

"For to this you were called, because Christ also suffered for us, leaving us an example, that you should follow His steps" (1 Peter 2:21 NKJV).

Day 27

The Falabella: A Carbon Copy

"Be imitators of God, therefore, as dearly loved children and live a life of love, just as Christ loved us and gave himself for us …."
(Ephesians 5: 1-2a NIRV)

Have you ever seen a horse about the size of a Great Dane? The Falabella is one of the smallest breeds in the world, averaging seven or eight hands. (Remember a hand is about four inches). The average Falabella is shorter than a yardstick. Because of his size, many people think he's a pony, but he's a miniature horse. A carbon copy of the bigger guys!

The Falabella's roots take him back to Andalusians and Iberian horses in Argentina, South America. In 1868, Patrick Newtall started a breeding program including local Criollo horses known for their stamina. When Newtall died, his son-in-law, Juan Falabella, added the bloodlines of Welsh Ponies, Shetland Ponies, and small Thoroughbreds. Thus, a consistently small horse named the "Falabella" emerged over the next century.

In 1940, Julio C. Falabella, a descendent of Juan, founded the Falabella Horse Breeders Association to preserve the breed. At first, he set the horse's height standard to no more than ten hands, but later other breeders set today's standard of about seven to eight hands.

By the early 1950s, horse lovers all over the world became interested in the fascinating little horse. The Falabella gained popularity with not only horse breeders but with royalty and celebrities, as well. These first miniatures arrived in the United States in 1962 when a winery in Etiwanda, California, purchased 12 stallions to drive small stagecoaches in parades. Most of the Falabella miniatures in the U.S. today came from those 12 horses.

Although the Falabellas are the size of ponies, the similarity ends there. Their body shape, sleek coat, and slim frame are very much like Thoroughbreds or Arabs. Falabellas have sturdy bones and a thick mane and tail. Their colors can be black, brown, bay, pinto, and palomino. Strangely, though, there are no Appaloosa-colored Falabellas.

If you think a full-grown Falabella is tiny, a foal is even smaller. If you measure something 24 inches high, you'll see how little the Falabellas are when they're born. As small as they are, it takes three years for them to mature.

You might wonder what anyone would do with horses so small. Because Falabellas have a calm, sweet temperament and train easily, they can be ridden by very young children. But the Falabellas have many other jobs, and they do them well! They drive carts, and some folks enter the little horses in shows. In recent years, Falabellas have worked jobs that have won the hearts of young and old alike. One of the horse's most valuable uses is being guide animals for special needs folks. Falabellas can also be trained as service animals, visiting children in hospitals or the elderly in senior centers.

No matter where the Falabellas live, even in extreme hot or cold, they thrive as much as their taller counterparts. What the big guys can do, the little horses can do, and just as well. You might say these miniatures are carbon copies of the bigger breeds.

A "carbon copy" is something or someone similar or almost identical to another. Has anyone ever said you're a carbon copy of your mother or father? That means you look just like one of them.

The Bible tells us we should strive to be carbon copies or imitators of the Lord Jesus Christ too. That means as we Christians grow in our faith and love for God, we'll become more like Jesus in our thoughts, words, and actions.

Have you ever thought you might be considered a carbon copy of Jesus? As you do your best to follow God and please Him, wouldn't it be great if those around you would think you were a carbon copy of Jesus? If you strive to love others as Jesus loves us, then it might just be the case.

PRAYER:

Dear God, I would love to be a carbon copy of my Savior Jesus Christ. Help me to live every day to please Him. In Jesus' name, amen.

SADDLE UP! (What would God have you do now?)

List two things Jesus did when He was on earth that showed how much He loved others. Decide how you can show that same love to others.

_____

_____

_____

_____

Take your ride: (Do you know?)

Since 1999, the Guide Horse Foundation has worked to provide miniature horses to the blind in rural areas.

Dismount and cool down your horse! (Do you know?)

"I tell you the truth, anyone who has faith in me will do what I have been doing ...." (John 14:12a NIRV)

Day 28

The Friesian: Majestic!

*"His glory is great in Your salvation; honor and majesty
You have placed upon him."
(Psalm 21:5 NKJV)*

Have you've noticed how many horses are named after places where they were first found? Friesians, sometimes called "Belgian Blacks," fit into this category. Considered one of the oldest breeds in Europe, the Friesian originated in Friesland, a province in northwest Netherlands. Although he has the strong build of a draft horse and looks like he'd only be used for pulling a plow, he's graceful and nimble. When he prances by in a parade, people can't help but admire how majestic he is.

As majestic as the Friesian appears to be now, it's believed that during the Middle Ages (the 5th to the 15th Centuries), his ancestors were used as war horses. The Friesians' husky size and strength enabled them to carry knights in heavy armor. During the 16th and 17th Centuries heavy war horses were no longer needed, so

Andalusians were crossbred with Friesians to produce a lighter horse for driving carriages.

Over the next 300 years, interest in the breed dropped, and Friesians nearly became extinct. Sadly, at the turn of the 20th Century, there were only three purebred stallions left. The breed struggled to survive, and then, contrary to so many other horses that declined during World War II, the Friesians made a strong comeback. Dutch farmers used them for transportation and farming due to fuel shortages.

Despite the Friesian's shaky roots, he's growing in numbers and popularity and performs in all kinds of harness and under saddle competition. Most recently, he's also making a strong showing in dressage events.

The most unusual fact about the Friesians is they must be black to be registered. However, their colors can also be black/bay, dark brown, and chestnut is sometimes allowed for mares and geldings. If there's any white at all on a Friesian, it can only be a small star on his forehead.

The Friesian stands at 14.2 to 17 hands. He has a beautiful arched neck and a muscular body with strong, sloping hindquarters. He has a long, thick mane and tail, which are often wavy, and his feet are feathered. He's known for a brisk, high-stepping trot. Although he's very energetic, he's also gentle and trains well.

Friesians come with two different body types—baroque (bah·roke), which has the more solid build of the first Friesians, and the finer-boned sport horse. Although both types are common, the sport horse has become more popular in the show ring.

Because of their gorgeous black coat, flowing mane and tail, arched neck, and high step, Friesians appear in many movies and TV shows, especially in fantasies. They remain calm and perform beautifully when being filmed, and they are stunning in their appearance. A Friesian tends to have great presence and to carry himself with royal elegance. Whether he's driving a fancy carriage or prancing under saddle, he can only be defined as majestic.

Anyone or anything that is "majestic" has a quality of dignity, beauty, and grandeur. The word "majesty" refers to someone who has great power or a high position. Have you ever heard someone call a king or queen "your majesty"?

The Bible tells us that Jesus is the Supreme Authority of the entire universe and heavens, and we should worship Him as the most powerful ruler of all. Someday King Jesus is coming back to earth on a white horse, and every Christian will have the privilege of bowing in person before Him and addressing Him as "Your Majesty." I can't wait for that time to come.

How about you? Is the Majestic God of the Universe the King of your life?

PRAYER:

Dear God, I want You to be the ruler of my life. I pray I'll be a loyal servant, willing to do whatever You ask of me. In Jesus' name, amen.

SADDLE UP! (What would God have you do now?)

Read Revelation 19:11-16 and write four titles of royalty Jesus Christ is called in those verses:

_____

_____

_____

Take your ride: (Do you know?)

Some Friesian events feature the horse driving a sjee, a cart with only two, but very large, wheels.

Dismount and cool down your horse! (Do you know?)

"To the only wise God our Saviour, be glory and majesty, dominion and power, both now and ever. Amen" (Jude 1:25).

Day 29

The Gypsy Vanner:
The Horse with Many Names

"Wherefore God also hath highly exalted him, and given him a name which is above every name: That at the name of Jesus every knee should bow, of things in heaven, and things in earth, and things under the earth."
(Philippians 2:9-10)

Gypsy Vanner Horses have gained popularity with horse lovers worldwide only recently. However, the Romani people (nomads) of Great Britain have known of this breed since the mid-19th Century. In fact, those travelers were instrumental in developing this special horse over the next fifty years. Through the crossbreeding of Dales Ponies (known as strong draft pullers), Fell Ponies, Shires, and Clydesdales, the short but stocky and powerful Gypsy horse emerged. The wandering groups finally had the perfect horse to pull their vardoes, also known as caravans (little houses on wheels).

A Gypsy Horse received special training to pull a vardo. Going up a steep hill, he had to learn to keep pulling the vardo until he reached the pinnacle; otherwise, because of the weight of the vardo, the horse might not have been able to get started again. During training, an old hat was sometimes placed on a frightened horse's head. That kept him from seeing backward over the top of his blinders at the wagon looming at his back and spooking him. Because the horse was so essential to the travelers, he was considered part of the family and interacted with even the children. Thus, only those Gypsies with calm temperaments became vardo horses.

The Gypsy has the body type of much larger draft horses with heavy bones and broad backs, but most of the breed only stands at 14 to 15 hands. He comes in all brown and black colors and all combinations of pinto. A major feature making the Gypsy so handsome is the long-flowing mane, tail, and impressive feathers on every leg from the hock down. Besides his amazing appearance, the Gypsy is friendly and willing to learn.

Gypsies are now being used in all kinds of events. They pull carts and carriages, perform in dressage and show jumping, and they've become popular western pleasure horses. Because of his sweet nature, he's also a wonderful family horse and is a great trail horse or therapy equine. In the U. S., the Gypsy horse is used in many equestrian sports and does quite well in combined driving and dressage. In 2001, a pair of Gypsies became grand champs in tandem driving team competition (one horse directly in back of the first horse, not side by side).

More interesting than the Gypsy Vanner's roots is the long list of names this horse has been given: Colored Cob, Gypsy Cob,

Irish Cob, Tinker Horse, Tinker Pony, Gypsy Horse, and, of course, the Gypsy Vanner. How in the world did this little horse get so many different names?

Founded in 1998, 2002, and 2003, three different groups of horse lovers, the Irish Cob Society, the Gypsy Cob and Drum Horse Association, and the Gypsy Cob Society of America all decided to refer to the breed as "Cob," the name they believed the Romani breeders used.

Gypsies are also called "Tinker Horses" or "Tinker Ponies." Those names originated with breed associations in the countries of Belgium, Sweden, and the Netherlands, where the Gypsies are listed in the Universal Equine Life Number database under the Tinker breed name.

In 2008, the newly incorporated Gypsy Horse Registry of America used the name "Gypsy Horse." However, this organization states that it recognizes all breed names in use today.

So how did the breed assume the most popular name, Gypsy Vanner?

As early as 1888, the term "vanner," had referred to a type of horse rather than to a certain breed. Since Gypsies originated as horses used for pulling vardoes or caraVANs, the name "Vanner" became associated with the breed.

In 1996, Gypsies made their way to the United States thanks to horse enthusiasts, Dennis and Cindy Thompson, who weren't sure the breed had a proper name. They had read about the name

"Vanner" being added to the horse's name in other countries, liked the name, and founded the Gypsy Vanner Horse Society that same year.

While the Gypsy Vanner has seven different names, do you know the Lord Jesus Christ has many more? The Bible tells us that Jesus has over a hundred different names, and every name exalts Him as the only true God and Savior.

Have you ever heard Jesus called "The Great Creator" or "The Good Shepherd"? How about "The Prince of Peace" or "The Son of God"? These are just a few of Jesus' many names, all displaying His wisdom, power, and love for us.

Do you have a favorite name for Jesus? No matter which name you choose as your favorite, always remember one of the most important names, "Savior," the one that offers eternal life to those who truly believe.

PRAYER:

Dear God, I realize that the names Jesus has all point to how great and wonderful He is. Thank you most of all, Jesus, for being my Savior. In Jesus' name, amen.

SADDLE UP!   (What would God have you do now?)

Read these verses in the Bible and write the names given to Jesus:

Isaiah 7:14

_____

_____

Hebrews 12:2

_____

_____

Revelation 1:8

_____

_____

Take your ride: (Do you know?)

Training a Gypsy to pull a vardo began at a very early age with the colt or filly tied with a short rope to the collar of the pulling horse then led along that horse's side.

Dismount and cool down your horse! (Do you know?)

"For unto us a child is born, unto us a son is given: and the government shall be upon his shoulder: and his name shall be called Wonderful, Counsellor, The mighty God, The everlasting Father, The Prince of Peace" (Isaiah 9:6).

Day 30

The Hackney Horse:
The Rolls Royce of Carriage Driving

"And He has on His robe and on His thigh a name written:
KING OF KINGS AND LORD OF LORDS."
(Revelation 19:16 NKJV)

The Hackney Horse is another superb breed that originated in Great Britain. He's not to be confused with the Hackney Pony, which can't be taller than 14.2 hands and has the usual characteristics of a pony, not a horse.

The first records of any Hackney Horse date back to the 14th Century in Norfolk (a county in eastern Great Britain) when the King of England, Edward III, required excellent trotting horses to be used for riding. Then in 1542, King Henry VIII ordered his wealthy subjects to breed only the very best trotting stallions.

With excellent crossbreeding in the late 17th to the early 18th Centuries, the Hackney developed from the Norfolk Trotter,

128

Yorkshire Roadster, the Arabian, and the Thoroughbred. Wow! What strong bloodlines this high stepper has! Before that time, heavier, big-boned horses pulled wagons, and they were in no hurry to do it. However, people wanted to get places faster, so they focused on lighter horses such as the Hackney. At first, folks simply admired the beauty of the Hackney but soon discovered his amazing trotting ability and seemingly endless energy. He could cover up to sixty miles in one day!

When people first entered Hackneys in competition, it was "under saddle" (a rider on the horse), not harness. As road conditions improved and the Hackney became the carriage horse, he then competed in harness. Thus, he became known as a riding and driving horse of great excellence.

During the 19th Century as with so many other driving breeds, the invention of modern machinery and the expansion of the railway endangered the carriage horses. Fortunately, Hackney owners revived the breed by selective crossbreeding with Norfolk and Yorkshire Trotters known for their style and speed. The impressive gaits of the Hackney Horse saved him from extinction and began his awesome appearance in England's show ring.

The Hackney first appeared in the United States in 1878 when a Hackney enthusiast, Alexander Cassatt, brought the first Hackney Pony to the United States. Because Hackneys came in both pony and horse height ranges, they were one of the few breeds that recognized both pony and horse sizes.

As the Hackney Pony developed in the late 19th Century, Hackney Horses were bred to different pony breeds in order to create a very specific type of show pony. In 1891 with the two breeds becoming increasingly distinct in their characteristics, Cassatt and other Hackney enthusiasts founded the American Hackney Horse Society now based in Lexington, Kentucky.

Over the last few decades, the Hackney's breeding has further produced a horse ideal for carriage driving. The Hackney Horse ranges in height from 14 to 15.3 hands. Their common colors are black, brown, bay and chestnut, and there are even some spotted ones. He has an elegant presence with a small head, well-shaped ears, and a natural high-set tail. But what is the Hackney most well-known for? Of course, his natural high-stepping gait! Although he's best known for stealing the show in harness, he can also give a smooth and exciting ride. A pleasant surprise is his outstanding ability in show jumping and dressage competition.

To bring the excellence of the Hackney to the world's horse enthusiasts, in 2003 the American Hackney Horse Society started the Open Competition Awards Program to recognize blue-ribbon Hackneys that were competing against other breeds.

Today proud owners compete in Carriage Driving and Coaching with their Hackney Horses, many driving away with top honors. Horse lovers often have to admit there's nothing more elegant than a Hackney driving a fancy antique carriage. Because of the Hackney's royal appearance, it's easy to understand that he's called the Rolls Royce of carriage driving.

Do you know what it means to label something a "Rolls Royce"?

The term "Rolls Royce" means the very best of something. A Rolls Royce car is one of the most expensive, special-made cars in the world. As the Hackney is labeled the Rolls Royce of carriage driving, our God and Savior, the Lord Jesus Christ, can be labeled the "Rolls Royce of all gods." He's not only the best God. He's the only true God.

Sadly, many people around the world worship gods that aren't even alive. They worship statues that can't hear or speak. Some cultures worship animals, believing their ancestors' souls live in the animals they worship. But saddest of all are the millions of people who believe they can go to heaven if they please their gods by being good or by doing kind deeds. But our one true God doesn't expect that from us. All our God asks is that we trust in His Son Jesus to be our Savior, the only one who can forgive all our sins.

If you've trusted in Jesus as your Savior, then you're believing in the Rolls Royce of gods, and you always can be sure of heaven when you die.

PRAYER:

Dear God, I thank Jesus my Savior for being the One True God, whom I can trust to go to heaven. I realize there are no other gods like Him anywhere. In Jesus' name, amen.

SADDLE UP! (What would God have you do now?)

List a few things that you think people might be doing to try to earn their way to heaven. Then thank God that you know that it's your faith in Christ that opens the way to eternal life.

_____

_____

_____

Take your ride: (Do you know?)

In the 1820s, a Hackney called "Norfolk Cob" was recorded as trotting two miles in just five minutes and four seconds.

Dismount and cool down your horse! (Do you know?)

"Who is like unto thee, O LORD, among the gods? who is like thee, glorious in holiness, fearful in praises, doing wonders?" (Exodus 15:11).

Day 31

The Haflinger: Always the Same

"Jesus Christ the same yesterday, and to day, and for ever."
(Hebrews 13:8)

Two theories about the origin of this handsome, friendly, and useful breed have surfaced in recent years.

Some horse enthusiasts believe Haflingers came from the Tyrolean Mountains in southern Austria and northern Italy, possibly as far back as medieval times. The breed's name, in fact, comes from the village of Hafling in northern Italy. (The Italian word for Hafling is "Avelignese" (Ah vale lig nee´ see), the name which some people call the Haflinger.)

Although people sometimes also refer to the Haflinger as a "mountain pony," he's a horse. Why was he sometimes called a pony? Perhaps because a type of light mountain pony was first found in the Tyrolean region. That little pony might have been the ancestor of the modern Haflinger.

The second theory is much more complicated, one that horse lovers might not want to take the time to figure out. Some believe the Haflinger descended from a stallion that Louis IV (the Holy Roman Emperor at that time) gave his son Prince Louis of Brandenburg (a city in northeast Germany) as a wedding gift in 1342.

Regardless of the Haflinger's start, the evidence points to his roots going back hundreds of years. His lineage has been traced to one of seven studs, a beautiful horse named Folie.

As the Haflinger developed over time, during the second half of the 20th Century breeders worked on his temperament, a very important quality of any good horse. Haflinger admirers considered the horse's attitude so important, they made a quiet, kind nature one of the official breed standards. Thus, no matter how handsome a Haflinger is, if he has a stubborn streak, he'll flunk an official inspection and be denied his registry.

Some horse organizations recognize two types of Haflingers. One is a shorter, heavier type used as a packhorse and for farm and forestry work for hundreds of years. Even today, the Austrian and German armies still uses Haflingers as packhorses in rough terrain such as the highest Alpines in their countries.

The other type is taller and lighter, used for light driving, under-saddle competition, and pleasure riding. Although they're very popular as dressage horses for children, they're still strong and tall enough to carry adults.

There are several national shows for Haflingers worldwide, including those in Germany, Great Britain, and the U. S. One very interesting fact that has nothing to do with riding a horse is that in Germany the Haflinger produces the majority of the horse milk consumed. How would you like to try some milk from such a handsome horse?

So, how handsome is the Haflinger? The Haflinger is an athletic and sturdy medium-sized horse. Up until the 1940s, he stood at 13.3 hands, but today he stands at between 13.2 and 15 hands. Haflinger breeders shy away from breeding horses shorter than 13.2 hands. However, if a Haflinger is taller than 15 hands, he can be registered if he meets other breed requirements. One of the most important requirements is this horse's eye-catching color.

You'll never see a black, white, or spotted Haflinger. This equine is always a chestnut color, the shades ranging from a light gold to a rich golden brown or liver. The mane and tail are always white or flaxen (pale grayish yellow.) So if you're looking for a Haflinger, focus on his color first because Haflingers' color is always the same and will never change.

Do you know something or someone else who's always the same and never changes?

The Bible tells us that we worship the one true God, who has been the same throughout eternity and will never change. That's good news for us! We can count on God to guide us with the same godly principles He set in motion from the beginning of time when

He created the earth and everything in it. He wrote all those principles we need to know in His Holy Word.

One thing God never changes his mind about is sin. Some people think they don't sin. They just think they make mistakes. But God's Word tells us that everyone has sinned. Because God can't tolerate sin, he will judge it.

However, the best news ever is that God hasn't changed his mind about how we can go to Heaven. From the beginning of time, He and His Only Son Jesus decided that Jesus would come to earth to save us from our sins. The decision they made thousands of years ago is still true today.

Aren't you glad God doesn't change? You can always trust all the promises in God's Word that point to salvation and give great peace in a believer's heart.

PRAYER:

Dear God, I'm so glad I can count on you to tell me how to live through your Holy Word that never changes Thank you for never changing. In Jesus' name, amen.

SADDLE UP! (What would God have you do now?)

Read the following verses and write what they tell us about something God never changes:

Psalm 33:4

_____

_____

John 3:16:

_____

_____

Philippians 4:7

_____

_____

Take your ride: (Do you know?)

At the end of the 20th Century, the army in India tried to use Haflingers to breed pack horses for mountain work, but the horses couldn't stand the hot climate, so the program failed.

Dismount and cool down your horse! (Do you know?)

"For I am the LORD, I change not..." (Malachi 3:6 a).

Day 32

The Hanoverian: Time Well Spent

"Redeeming the time, because the days are evil."
(Ephesians 5:16)

The country of Germany has the reputation of breeding many of the finest horses in the world. Among those breeds, the warm-blooded Hanoverian is arguably the most popular or famous. Like so many other horses named after the region where they were first found, this beautiful equine is from Hanover in northern Germany. He's often seen in the Olympic Games and other world class competitive English riding styles. Although his roots branded him as a carriage driver, he's now known as one of the outstanding competitive show horses. His lineage and excellence in performance can be attributed to only one fact: the time spent by Hanoverian enthusiasts to breed and train such an outstanding horse.

The Hanoverians' roots go back to 1714 when King George I of England sent some of his finest Thoroughbreds to Germany where they were crossbred with Germany's native horses. Then in 1735, his son, George II, developed a special stallion to pilot a breeding program of superb working horses and dependable cavalry mounts. At first, he used black Holsteiners (a taller athletic German horse) then added Thoroughbred blood. The newer Hanoverian became more nimble and highly skilled for competition. Through the 1700s, the developing Hanoverian was also crossbred with Cleveland Bays, Neapolitans, Andalusians, Prussians, and Mecklenburgs. The result? A first-class coach horse used for hundreds of years.

Fast forward to the 1940s. Horse enthusiasts started the world-wide search for an excellent sport horse that could also serve as a general riding mount. Again, Hanoverian breeders answered the call by crossbreeding their stock with Thoroughbreds. However, occasionally using Anglo-Arabian or Trakehner studs produced the beautiful champion Hanoverian we now see winning blue ribbons all around the world.

The Hanoverian of today has a teachable temperament with a strong back, powerful body, and strong legs. He stands between 15.3 and 17.2 hands, and his color is usually chestnut, bay, black, and gray. Registered Hanoverians can't have too much white anywhere on their bodies, and buckskin, palomino and cremello horses are ineligible for registration.

Since the Hanoverian is bred for the specialties of jumping and dressage, his haunches must be powerful, enabling him to cover the terrain with plenty of spring and force. He has won dozens of gold medals in all three equestrian Olympic competitions: dressage, show jumping, and eventing. The eventing class is considered the most demanding of all for both horse and rider. It originated with well-trained cavalry horses, which had to cover rough terrain and obstacles while running at full speed. As the eventing class evolved over time, it also included dressage and show jumping as well as cross country jumping and galloping.

The Hanoverians are so highly trained, they can be priced at high as $60,000 or more. If you'd like to go shopping for a Hanoverian, you can easily identify him by an "H" brand on his left hindquarter. You'll also spot two numbers under the brand, the last two digits of the horse's registration number.

Because of the time spent over hundreds of years to produce this champion, the Hanoverian is strong and elegant, an equine athlete full of grace and beauty. I would say that's been time well spent, wouldn't you?

Have you discovered in your daily routine that anything worthwhile takes lots of time? It takes time to put a thousand-piece jigsaw puzzle together. It takes time to do any chores well. It takes time to do schoolwork, and after years and years of studying, you'll finally graduate from high school. Most importantly, it takes time to become a strong Christian.

Speaking of time well spent, do you ever think going to church, reading the Bible, and praying is time well spent, or do you think it's a waste of time?

As usual, the Bible has something to say about your time and how you should spend it. God wants you to draw closer to Him and become a strong Christian. The only way that can happen is if you *do* spend time going to church, reading the Bible, and praying. Now that's time well spent!

PRAYER:

Dear God, please help me to spend my time wisely. I want to learn more about you because you're such a wonderful God. In Jesus' name, amen.

SADDLE UP! (What would God have you do now?)

Write some activities you know waste time and decide to use your time more wisely:

_____

_____

_____

_____

_____

Take your ride: (Do you know?)

One of the highest prices ever paid for a Hanoverian was $1,125,000 (That's one million, one hundred, twenty-five thousand dollars) for the purchase of a horse named Lemony's Nicket.

Dismount and cool down your horse! (Do you know?)

"He has made everything beautiful in its time. He has also set eternity in the hearts of men; yet they cannot fathom what God has done from beginning to end" *(Ecclesiastes 3:11a NIRV).*

Lady was a good old girl.

Day 33

The Icelandic Horse: A National Treasure!

"But we have this treasure in earthen vessels,
that the excellency of the power may be of God, and not of us."
(2 Corinthians 4:7)

Can you guess where the Icelandic horse has his roots? If you said Iceland, you are correct. Do you know where Iceland is?

Iceland is a small, island (considered a country of Europe) not too far from Greenland in the North Atlantic Ocean where the weather can be frigid and downright nasty. Despite the climate, Icelandic horses are easy to keep and very hardy, and the bitter cold temperatures don't bother him at all. The reason? They have a double coat for extra insulation.

The Icelandic horse's beginnings date back to the 9th and 10th Centuries when Norsemen (Scandinavian Vikings) settled on Iceland and brought their ponies with them. If you check the Icelandic historical records and literature, you'll find the breed mentioned often, the first reference as early as the 12th Century. Because the Norse settlers honored their horses and brought their Norse mythology and traditions with them, the Icelanders of today have their "very own horse," which they consider a treasure.

Although the Icelandic has the characteristics and height of a pony, the cute little guy is considered a horse. Several theories have emerged as to why Icelandics are always called horses, among them the breed's spirited temperament and friendly personality. Although they only weigh between 730 and 840 pounds and stand at 13 to 14 hands, breed registries always refer to Icelandics as horses. They also have heavier bones and are able to carry tremendous weights, which suggest a "horse" classification.

A very unique trait of the Icelandic is his amazing coat colors. The breed comes in all different shades, over 100 in all, including dun, bay, black, gray, palomino, pinto and roan. Along with the variety of colors, the Icelandic adds to his attractive looks with a full mane and flowing tail. Another unique trait the Icelandic has is two extra gaits in addition to the walk, trot, and canter that other breeds all have. Thus, he's often called a "five-gaited horse."

Although the Icelandic is the only horse on Iceland, he's also popular in many countries in Europe and North America. One reason is that in 1904, Icelandic enthusiasts created the first breed society for the Icelandic horse. Today the breed is represented by Icelandic organizations in 19 different nations, organized by the International Federation of Icelandic Horse Associations.

Another reason for his popularity is his long life. An Icelandic mare in Denmark reached a record age of 56. Another one in Great

Britain lived 42 years. The breed's long years can partially be due to the lack of exposure to diseases from other horses in Iceland. Icelandic law prevents equines from coming into the country, and exported ones can't return.

Although the Icelandics are not usually ridden until they're four years old and they don't reach full maturity until age seven, the people of Iceland love them and are proud of them for several reasons. Because Iceland is so remote, the horses have remained a pure breed, unchanged for over 1,000 years. The horses aren't easily spooked, probably because they have no natural predators. They're friendly and calm, although they're also spunky and confident. The people have also used them for all kinds of tasks, including sheep herding, pleasure riding, racing, and showing. It's very easy to understand why the people consider their little horse a national treasure.

I'm sure you know a treasure is something extremely valuable. Some people, like archeologists, search the world over for treasures from past civilizations. However, Christians have a treasure that's far more valuable than any ancient relic like gold or precious jewels.

The Bible tells us when we accept Jesus as our Savior, God gives us power to live for Him. The power comes from the Holy Spirit, who lives inside of us. If we want to please God, the Holy Spirit helps us to do our best. That power is the treasure to help us live for Jesus.

The Bible also tells us about another kind of treasure, the kind that we have in our possession. Whether you're rich or poor, there are some things you own that you might consider your "treasure." It might be money. Maybe it's a collection of model cars. Maybe it's your computer or smart phone. A personal treasure can be anything of value to that person. According to the Bible, whatever treasure you focus on and spend a lot of time on, that's where your heart will be, as well.

Have you ever thought that God...or your Bible could be a treasure? If you value them more than anything you own, then your heart's in the right place.

PRAYER:

Dear God, thank you for the treasure of the Bible and You in my life. I pray that I can always focus my heart on You as my most valuable treasure. In Jesus' name, amen.

SADDLE UP! (What would God have you do now?)

Write the name of any possessions you have that you consider "treasures." Then decide if you love those things more than God.

_____

_____

_____

_____

_____

Take your ride: (Do you know?)

In the 1780s, many of the Icelandic Horses died following a volcanic eruption at Laki in southeast Iceland, mostly by eating fluorine-contaminated grass or by starving.

Dismount and cool down your horse! (Do you know?)

"For where your treasure is, there will your heart be also" (Luke 12:34).

Day 34

The Highland Pony: Willing to Serve

"Also I heard the voice of the Lord, saying, Whom shall I send, and who will go for us? Then said I, Here am I; send me."
(Isaiah 6:8)

To find the Highland Pony, hop on a plane in Iceland and fly about 600 miles southeast to Scotland, a country that's part of the United Kingdom in Europe. The Icelanders have their Icelandic Horse; the Scots have their Highland Pony!

The Highland Pony is one of three breeds from the Scottish Highlands and Islands along with the Shetland Pony and the predominantly gray Eriskay (Er´ is kay) Pony. In the 16th Century, French and Spanish explorers brought horses, including Percherons (heavy draft horses), to Scotland. In the 19th Century, crossbreeding with Hackneys, Fell Ponies, and Dales Ponies gave us the Highland of today.

Because this pony survived in a tough environment of mountains and moorlands for several hundred years, he's the largest and strongest of the native ponies in the British Isles. (A moorland is an upland habitat with low-growing vegetation on acidic soils.) The Scots soon discovered that, besides the Highland being tough and hardy, he rarely needed shoes, and he was easy to keep. Therefore, even though the pony only stands between 13 and 14.2 hands, he became a valuable member of the workforce for farmers and lumberjacks. He also became a prized pack animal, carrying a hunter's kill that often weighed 200 pounds. The Scots called him an "all-rounder" and valued him greatly because of his willingness to work hard, his surefootedness, and his strength.

The Highland Pony Society has strict color restrictions on its special horse; yet the pony's colors are quite numerous. He's mainly dun, but he can be gray, brown, black, and a dark chestnut. He can have a stripe and zebra markings on the legs along with soft, silky feathering on his feet. Other acceptable colors include "mouse," "yellow," cream dun, and red dun.

A coloring mark unique to the Highland is what's called a "transverse stripe," a streak of dark hair that crosses over the withers on both sides of the pony's body. Colors such as pinto are not allowed. Stallions with white markings other than a small star on the forehead can't be licensed by the Highland Pony Society, and no white markings other than a star, white legs, or white hooves are allowed in the Highland Pony show ring. Regardless of his coat color, the Highland must always have a flaxen mane and tail, which make his appearance quite handsome.

Over the centuries, the Highland has adapted to the often severe climate of Scotland, mostly due to his amazing coat very similar to the Icelandics. The Highland's winter coat consists of a waterproof layer of strong, thick hair over a softer yet dense undercoat. (The waterproof coat came from his Eriskay Pony.) When the coat sheds in the spring, a smoother summer coat emerges. Although the Highland is known for his toughness and hardiness, those traits are balanced by a kind attitude and easy-going temperament, willing to do whatever he's asked. And he's asked to do a lot!

Today the Highlands still work hard on farms in Scotland but are also valued as a prized family pony. His other uses include logging, hauling deer carcasses from the hills, and trekking (trail riding sometimes for several days).

Wow, look at all the jobs this little pony can do! Would you agree the Highland has a willing spirit to do anything his owner asks of him? What a sweet and kind attitude he has. He has what we call a "servant's heart"!

Would you say that you have a servant's heart? Are you willing to do whatever is asked of you with a sweet attitude? How about your schoolwork? Your chores around the house?

If you love Jesus and want to please Him, then you might have a servant's heart. Someone with a servant's heart is willing to do whatever God asks of Him. Even at your young age, you can pray and ask God if He wants to use you in a special way when you grow up.

You're never too young to start being a Christian with a servant's heart.

PRAYER:

Dear God, today I give my life to you for service. I'm willing to do anything and go anywhere to ask of me. I thank Jesus for giving His own life for me. In Jesus' name, amen.

SADDLE UP! (What would God have you do now?)

Write what you'd be willing to do for God when you grow up. Write some things you could do now because you love Jesus and are thankful for his salvation:

_____

_____

_____

_____

_____

_____

Take your ride: (Do you know?)

There are only about 5,500 Highlands in the world today, most of them in Europe. Despite how popular the Highland is, he's still categorized as "At Risk" by horse experts.

Dismount and cool down your horse! (Do you know?)

"And whatsoever you do, do it heartily, as to the Lord, and not unto men; Knowing that of the Lord ye shall receive the reward of the inheritance: for ye serve the Lord Christ" (Colossians 3: 23-24).

The Kentucky Mountain Saddle Horse:
A Rule Follower

"And let the peace of God rule in your hearts,
to the which also ye are called in one body; and be ye thankful."
(Colossians 3:15)

The Kentucky Mountain Saddle Horse is a breed from ___?___ You guessed it, the state of Kentucky. This fabulous horse probably has his roots in smooth-gaited horses from the southeastern United States and the now-extinct Narragansett Pacer. He's related to the Tennessee Walking Horse and other gaited breeds, but, unfortunately, the exact details of his beginnings are unknown.

The Kentucky Mountain Saddle Horse has a similar history to the Rocky Mountain Horse. These two breeds are sometimes called "Mountain Pleasure Horses." Plantation owners looking for a powerful work horse developed the Kentucky Mountain Saddle Horse, which could also offer a comfortable, safe ride to the family members. Breeding eventually produced this equine's gentle temperament. He became the perfect mount not only for long travel over rough terrain but also for frequent family use. Even today, the breed has the reputation of being an excellent riding horse as well as a reliable mount for rugged trail riding.

This amazing horse rides "rocking chair smooth" for one reason. He has a natural ambling gait, which is completely different from the trot of most other breeds. The rider experiences smoothness because the horse always has at least one foot on the ground when he's "ambling."

Interest in the breed increased throughout the 20th Century, and in 1989, the Kentucky Mountain Saddle Horse Association (KMSHA) started. Because of the popularity of the breed with excessive white markings and pinto colors, in 2002 an additional Spotted Mountain Horse Association (SMHA) started to register Kentucky Mountain Saddle Horses with a lot of white. Thus, there are two different registries today: one for "solid" horses and one for pintos.

Because the history and lineage of the Kentucky Mountain Saddle Horse is not known, the two associations did extensive studies and formed detailed guidelines that any horse must follow to be registered as a Saddle Horse. Space doesn't allow for the listing of pages of all the rules and regulations, but let's take a look at a few:

1.   A Kentucky Mountain Saddle Horse must stand above 11 hands to be registered. Taller horses are divided into two

categories: Class A horses stand taller than 14.2 hands while Class B horses stand at 11 to 14.1 hands.

2. A horse registered with the Kentucky Mountain Saddle Horse Association can be all solid colors with white markings allowed on the face, legs, and small patches on the belly no larger than the size of the palm of a hand.

3. A horse with excessive white, including a full white face, white above the knees or hocks, or any pinto markings must register with the Spotted Mountain Horse Association.

4. The horse must have a flat facial profile, a mid-length, well-arched neck, a deep chest and well-sloped shoulders.

5. The horse must display a gentle temperament and willing disposition. Any horse that is unruly or unmanageable will not be accepted for certification.

6. The horse must have a smooth, comfortable, and natural four beat under saddle.

7. The horse may be barefoot or have shoes on all four hooves.

The Kentucky Mountain Saddle Horse certainly has to follow a ton of rules to be a member of his exclusive club!

How would you like to be a member of a family or a club with so many rules? What if you had to have purple hair or weigh two hundred pounds to be a member of your family? What if you had to get all A's in every test you take in school to pass to the next grade?

You probably think those rules just mentioned are ridiculous. But God has given us many good rules in the Bible, which help us live a successful and happy life. Some of those rules are the Ten Commandments, which are a guide for us to follow.

However, some people believe that by following the Ten Commandments they can work their way to heaven. Sadly, they also believe they have to follow a long list of other rules to win God's favor, and then He'll let them into Heaven. But that's not what the Bible says. Once we've accepted Jesus as our Savior, heaven is promised to us. All the rules God has given us are to be used as a guide to help us live the Christian life.

Remember, there are good rules your parents and teachers have set to help you grow into a responsible, happy adult. And there are good rules God has given you to help you grow into a responsible, happy Christian. Always thank Jesus that He made the way to heaven with his sacrifice on the cross, and you don't have to try to keep a lot of rules to get there.

PRAYER:

Dear God, help me obey the rules You and others in my life have set for me. I know they're for my good. In Jesus' name, amen.

SADDLE UP! (What would God have you do now?)

Write some rules your parents or teachers have that you think are for your good. Determine to obey them the best you can:

_____

_____

_____

_____

_____

Take your ride: (Do you know?)

The Kentucky Mountain Saddle Horse is the member of an exclusive club of more than thirty horse breeds that are "gaited," able to perform a four-beat ambling gait.

Dismount and cool down your horse! (Do you know?)

"I have longed for thy salvation, O LORD; and thy law is my delight" (Psalm 119:174).

Day 36

The Lipizzan: He and his Rider are One!

*believe these works. Then you will know
and understand that the Father is in me
"...   and I am in the Father."
(John 10:38b NIRV)*

The Lipizzan is one of the most beautiful horses in God's creation. He's known as "the dancer" and is considered the ambassador of all the fancy horse performances: classical dressage.

The dressage this equine has perfected is completely different from what you see in the familiar dressage performance in a horse show or the Olympics. The Lipizzan, with powerful haunches, performs high jumping and kicking movements such as the piaffe (pee´ af) and passage (pass sahg´). Strange as it seems, the Lipizzan was specifically bred for an ancient art form that began as training for cavalry mounts.

The Lipizzan's roots go back to the Muslim Moors, who occupied Spain from about 711 to 1492 and considered the Spanish horses the supreme cavalry mount. By the 16th Century, when the

Habsburgs ruled Spain and Austria, they wanted to develop a powerful but agile horse for the military and for use in the popular riding schools for the European nobility. In 1562, Habsburg Emperor Maximillian II brought the Spanish Andalusian horse to Austria. In 1580, his brother, Archduke Charles II, perfected a similar stud near the village of Lipizza (now called Lipica) in Slovenia (a small country just south of Austria).

The White Stallions of Vienna at the Spanish Riding School in Austria came from that lineage. The Lipizzans, (only stallions), still train at the world-renowned school to learn the complicated and beautiful movements called "airs above the ground." The horses arrive when they're four years old and train an average of six years. They graduate when they've mastered all the skills required to perform perfectly before large audiences all around the world. Despite their demanding work, Lipizzans are an extremely hardy breed. Some have been able to perform the difficult exercises well into their 20s and have lived into their 30s.

Over the last century, the breed has been endangered numerous times by wars in Europe. Fortunately, horse enthusiasts have stepped in every time and rescued them. The most famous rescue occurred during World War II by General George S. Patton and our American troops. The 1963 Disney movie "Miracle of the White Stallions" made that rescue famous. Besides being featured in the Disney movie, Lipizzans have also starred or played supporting roles in many movies, TV shows, and books. In 2005, the Spanish

Riding School toured the U.S. to celebrate the 60th anniversary of Patton's rescue.

Today, all Lipizzans standing between 14 and 16 hands trace their bloodlines to eight stallions. Various breed registries also recognize 35 mare lines. The majority of horses, 11,000 in 19 countries, are registered through the Lipizzan International Federation. Most Lipizzans are in Europe, but small numbers can be found in the Americas, Africa, and Australia.

Watching a performing Lipizzan, you'd think he's pure white. However, most Lipizzans are not true white horses. They're gray. Like all grays, they have black skin, dark eyes, and a coat that looks white. They're born dark—usually bay or black—and become lighter each year until they're between six and ten years old.

Because the Lipizzans are the only breed of horse developed in Slovenia, the Slovenians are proud to call the Lipizzan their national animal. They've even honored the horse by featuring a pair of Lipizzans on the 20-cent Slovenian euro coins.

Who can blame the people of Slovenia when considering their amazing dancing Lipizzans? If you ever have the privilege to see the Lipizzans in person, you'll probably sit in awe of their magnificent performance. But those horses didn't just happen to be that way.

The Lipizzans perform at the whim of skilled riders who, with the slightest signal of their hands or feet, direct the horses to execute their moves. Each horse and his rider move so perfectly together, they appear as one body, stunning the audiences with their spectacular maneuvers.

There are three important persons who also work together as one unit, and that's God the Father, Jesus Christ the Son, and the Holy Spirit. Many times in the scriptures, Jesus claimed that He and God are one. Therefore, Jesus claimed to be God, and rightfully so. We can't fully understand what Jesus meant when He said that He is one with God, but the Bible says to believe in faith that it's true.

Sadly, many people in the world today think Jesus was just a good man or a prophet of God, but not the Son of God, who is equal with God. If that were the case, Jesus couldn't be our Savior because only a perfect sacrifice can forgive our sins and make us ready for heaven.

If you believe that God the Father, the Holy Spirit, and Jesus the Son are "one" and that Jesus is your Savior, then you are on your way to heaven. With all the miracles Jesus performed on earth, how could He be anyone other than God in the flesh? Thank Him for being your Savior.

PRAYER:

Dear God, although I might not understand how You, the Holy Spirit, and Jesus can be "one," I believe it by faith. Thank you, Jesus, for coming to earth and dying for my sins. In Jesus' name, amen.

SADDLE UP!   (What would God have you do now?)

Read the following verses in the Bible and write the miracle Jesus performed:

Matthew 14: 15- 21

_____

_____

Mark 3: 1-5

_____

_____

John 11: 14, 38-44

_____

_____

Take your ride: (Do you know?)

The Spanish Riding School has a long-standing tradition to have at least one bay Lipizzan stallion in the stables, continued through the present day.

Dismount and cool down your horse! (Do you know?)

"I and My Father are one" (John 10:30).

Day 37

The Lusitano: Same Horse, Different Name

"...And the disciples were called Christians first in Antioch."
(Acts 11:26b)

Although cave paintings in the Iberian Peninsula (Portugal and Spain) have revealed the presence of horses there for thousands of years, the Lusitano from Portugal is one of the breeds "officially created" in recent time. The registry name of this breed is Puro Sangue Lusitano (Pure´oh San´gwee Lou sah tan´ oh), the Latin name for Portugal. But he's also known as the Portuguese, Peninsular, National, or Betico-lusitano horse. What's quite strange about the Lusitano is he originated as an Andalusian. A Portuguese Andalusian.

The Andalusians have their roots back to 711 A.D. when the Muslim Moors invaded the Iberian Peninsula and brought Barb horses with them. The Moors crossbred their steeds with the native horses and developed an equine useful for war, bull fighting, and even dressage. This new horse became a favorite of the

Conquistadors, who introduced him in the Americas between the 16th to the 18th Centuries. Known as "the Iberian war horse," that ancestor of the Lusitano served in battle as well as at important riding academies throughout Europe.

The Portuguese Andalusian and the Spanish Andalusian have had very similar characteristics for hundreds of years. However, in 1966, the Portuguese breeders wanted to develop their own horse, an even more nimble yet strong equine with the ability to move quickly around a charging bull in the bullfighting ring. (In Portuguese bullfighting, the bull is not killed.) Thus, the breeders split the Portuguese and Spanish stud books of the Andalusians, and the Portuguese one became known as the Lusitano, after the word "Lusitania," the ancient Roman name for Portugal.

The Lusitano horses' heights range from 15 to 15.3 hands. They can be any solid color including black, dun, and palomino but are usually gray, chestnut, or bay. They have a Roman nose, which is stouter than a more refined "dish face" you see on breeds like the Arabian. Because of the heavy work they're called to do, the Lusitanos have great muscle strength and agility; yet, they're intelligent and very willing to please.

Today's Lusitanos are very versatile. They've built quite a reputation for dressage, winning medals in several Olympics and World Equestrian Games over the last few years as part of Portuguese and Spanish dressage teams. They also have done well in driving competitions with a Belgian team of Lusitanos winning many international awards.

The breed is still used in bloodless bullfighting today, where it is expected that neither horse nor bull will be injured. Horses bred for this sport must be agile and calm, and when confronted by the bull, they must "keep their head." Much of the horse's and rider's safety depends on the skill of the horse and his ability to avoid the charging bull. In fact, it's considered a disgrace to the rider if the horse is injured in any way.

Today Lusitanos are found mostly in Portugal and Brazil, but they can be found in many other countries including Australia, Great Britain, South Africa, some European countries, and the U.S. Between 1980 and 1987, Lusitanos were even used for breeding Colorado Ranger horses, but today those crosses are no longer allowed by the breed registry.

With the popularity of this breed worldwide just in recent years, we should not forget his roots. Andalusian. Thanks to Portuguese horse enthusiasts, the Portuguese Andalusian breed, now called the Lusitano, became stronger and more nimble. What we now have is the same but improved horse with a different name!

Do you realize that people sometimes change their names for different reasons? God also has a special name for those who decide to love and serve Him. The Bible says that, although we might appear to be the same on the outside, when we accept Jesus as our Savior, we become "improved" on the inside, and we are then called

Christians. Being improved means we now have the Holy Spirit living inside us, and He helps us to do what's right and to say no to sin.

Have you asked Jesus to save you and make you ready for heaven? If so, do your family and friends call you a Christian? If you honor the Lord Jesus by your attitude and actions, then you'll be known as a Christ follower or a Christian.

PRAYER:

Dear God, help me to have the right attitude and actions so that my family and friends will have no trouble calling me a Christian. In Jesus' name, amen.

SADDLE UP! (What would God have you do now?)

Besides the name "Christian," think of a few other names you'd like to be called (Example: "kind," "friendly"). Do your attitude and actions merit those names?

_____

_____

_____

_____

Take your ride: (Do you know?)

The bond between early Iberian people and their horses was so strong, it's believed the original fables about the centaur (half man/half horse creature) originated in the Iberian Peninsula.

Dismount and cool down your horse! (Do you know?)

"The Lord knoweth them that are his. And, let every one that nameth the name of Christ depart from iniquity" (2 Timothy 2:19b).

Day 38

The Miniature Horse: No Doubt He's for Real!

*"I'm writing these things to you who believe in the name of the Son of God.
I'm writing so you will know that you have eternal life."*
(1 John 5:13 NIRV)

Here's a beautiful little equine that, although he's tiny, is the exact replica of the larger horse breeds. In fact, he's so much like the big guys, if you'd see a Miniature Horse standing in a pasture somewhere, you might think he's just a statue of a larger horse.

The Miniature Horse is just that—a horse, not a pony. We can trace his history back to the 17th Century in Europe when kings and nobles admired such different horses and sought to raise them. But many other Miniature Horses, or "Minis," who weren't fortunate enough to live in a king's barn worked as "pit ponies" inside mines. Sometimes those poor little horses lived inside the mines and never saw the light of day. The English began using ponies in their mines after the Mines and Collieries Act of 1842 prohibited the use of young children.

The first small horses in the United States date back to 1861, when a tiny-horse enthusiast, John Rarey, brought four Shetland Ponies, one only 24 inches tall, to our country. Throughout the late 1800s and into mid-1900, more Minis came from English and Dutch mines to work in coal mines in the U.S. Then in the 1960s, horse lovers as well as the general public developed a real interest in Miniature Horses, which, fortunately, brought the Minis out of the mines and into sport and show competition.

Over the years as more interest grew in the Minis, they were crossbred with other breeds such as the Hackney for a more handsome look and more nimble footwork. Although almost all Minis can't be ridden even by children, they're still very popular and are used in all kinds of competition such as driving, obstacle courses, and halter. Because they're so small, easy to keep, and interact well with humans, many Minis have important jobs. They're often kept as family pets, (although the Minis still have "horse" traits), and they also can be trained as service animals, doing the same things that dogs do who work for folks with special needs.

So how tiny is tiny? Take a yardstick and stand it on end. That's about the height of a Miniature Horse. Because they're so small, they're measured in inches not in hands. Any color or combination of colors is acceptable, so Minis come in a large variety of splashy colors, including palomino, pinto, and even a cross between a pinto and an Appaloosa called a "Pintaloosa."

You can find two registries in the United States for Miniature Horses, the American Miniature Horse Association (AMHA) and the American Miniature Horse Registry (AMHR). Founded in 1978, the AMHA started establishing the Miniature Horse as a distinct breed. Today there are dozens of miniature horse registries all over the world. Some of the registries want the breeding of Minis to keep horse characteristics, while other associations want their Minis to have pony characteristics. Along with all these different general Miniature Horse associations, there are also registries for specific types of Minis, such as the Falabella and the South African Miniature Horse.

Minis are healthy animals, often living longer than some full-sized horses. The average life span of Miniature Horses is from 25 to 35 years. Minis have become so popular all around the world that their associations have more than 12,000 enthusiasts in over 30 countries. For those Mini lovers, there's no doubt the little equine is a horse in every sense of the word.

Doubt. In our lives, doubt can surface at any time. Have you ever doubted it would stop raining for the family picnic? Or have you doubted whether you'd like the new broccoli casserole or not? Maybe you've doubted if you'd ever finish your tons of homework in one evening. Or maybe you've doubted if you'll ever get that puppy or pair of sneakers you want so badly. But there's one thing you should never doubt.

The Bible tells us when we accept Jesus as our Savior we should never doubt our salvation. When we become Christians, that doesn't mean we'll never sin or make mistakes again. It also doesn't mean we aren't Christians anymore. All God wants us to do is ask for forgiveness, and He does forgive. God's Word says we only ever have to ask Christ into our lives one time, and from that moment on, we never have to doubt that we are Christians ever again.

PRAYER:

Dear God, thank you for giving me eternal life that can never be taken away from me. In Jesus' name, amen.

SADDLE UP! (What would God have you do now?)

Write anything that might cause you to doubt whether you're a Christian or not. Ask God to forgive you, and He will. Remember, once a Christian, always a Christian.

_____

_____

_____

_____

_____

_____

Take your ride: (Do you know?)

The AMHA has nearly 230,000 registered Miniatures.

Dismount and cool down your horse! (Do you know?)

"But as for you, continue in what you have learned and have become convinced of, because you know those from whom you learned it, and how from infancy you have known the holy Scriptures, which are able to make you wise for salvation through faith in Christ Jesus" (2 Timothy 3: 14-15 NIRV).

Author's father with Suzy,
definitely not a mini.

Day 39

The Missouri Fox Trotter: Dependable

"Thy word is true from the beginning."
(Psalm 119:160a)

When farmers, plantation owners, and ranchers started settling our newly formed United States, they looked for a hardy, muscular horse that could do ranch work yet take the family members on a dependable trail ride. So in the early 1800s, the settlers of the Ozarks in Missouri developed a sure-footed horse that could perform work including working cattle, plowing fields, and hauling logs. But that same horse had to serve as the family's fancy buggy and riding horse in the evening's activities.

The Missouri Fox Trotter, developed from horses from Kentucky, Tennessee, and Virginia, filled that need to the "T." Crossbreeding with Arabians, Tennessee Walking Horses, Morgans, American Saddlebreds, and Standardbreds made the Trotter smoother and stronger. This versatile equine, able to travel great distances at a comfortable five- to-eight miles an hour, made the

Missouri Fox Trotting Horse a favorite of the country doctor, sheriff, traveling preacher, and rancher. In just a short time, the gaited Trotter gained notoriety for his stamina and smooth gaits.

In 1948, Trotter enthusiasts founded the Missouri Fox Trotting Horse Breed Association (MFTHBA) in Ava, Missouri with an open stud book that registered all horses with the fox trot gait and other specified physical characteristics describing the horse. Interest around the world grew, and the first Fox Trotters were exported to Europe in the 1950s when the Queen of England imported several palomino Trotters. The breed's popularity increased to the point that Missouri Fox Trotters are now seen throughout the United States, as well as in Canada and several European countries. As of 2012 the MFTHBA had registered over 97,000 horses with over 8,000 members. It's no surprise that the state of Missouri thinks highly of this unique equine. He's so special that in 2002, the state honored the Missouri Fox Trotter by naming him the official state horse of Missouri.

Missouri Fox Trotters come in all colors, including spotted and buckskin. You'll often see them with white facial and leg markings. They're muscular and have sloped shoulders, a short back, and sturdy legs. They stand at 14 to 16 hands and weigh between 900 and 1,200 pounds.

Today the Missouri Fox Trotting Horse is known as everyone's pleasure horse because of his gentle disposition and dependable, comfortable ride. He's most known today for his ambling gait, the "fox trot," a four-beat smooth gait in which the front foot of the diagonal pair lands before the hind pair. He's in demand for use in all kinds of show classes including pleasure, trail riding, endurance, and cross country. Because of his surefootedness and endurance in rough countryside, he's used by hunters and National Forestry Service rangers. You can often spot him in movies because of his gentle nature and willingness to work. Handicapped riding programs also use him because his smooth gait has proven to be beneficial for riders with minor physical disabilities. Wow! Would you agree "dependable" describes the Missouri Fox Trotter better than any other word?

Are you "dependable" like the Missouri Fox Trotter? If you're dependable, you can be trusted to complete tasks you're asked to do. Would your parent or teacher say you are dependable, or do you forget to do jobs you're asked to do? A Christian should be dependable because the God we love and serve is dependable.

The Bible tells us that we can depend on Jesus to be our Savior. He shed His blood and died on the cross to save anyone who believes in Him. The Bible is also dependable. Every word of it is true, which tells us about our wonderful God and the home in heaven we'll have one day. We have a God on whom we can depend.

PRAYER:

Dear God, thank you for being the God I can depend on. I also thank you for the Bible that tells me that believing in Jesus as my Savior makes me ready for heaven. In Jesus' name, amen.

SADDLE UP! (What would God have you do now?)

Write some responsibilities your parent or teacher might want you to do. Then decide to be dependable and finish the tasks on time.

_____

_____

_____

_____

_____

_____

Take your ride: (Do you know?)

Fox Trotters were the first horses to carry riders down the north rim of the Grand Canyon.

Dismount and cool down your horse! (Do you know?)

"Let your conduct be without covetousness; be content with such things as you have. For He Himself has said, "I will never leave you nor forsake you" *(Hebrews 13:5 NKJV).*

Author's first horse, Moon Doggie

Day 40

The Morgan: A Firm Foundation

"For other foundation can no man lay than that is laid, which is Jesus Christ."
(1Corinthians 3:11)

<u>Justin Morgan Had a Horse</u>. Have you ever read Marguerite Henry's book with that title about the man whose horse started the Morgan breed?

Here's another horse breed named after a person. The Morgan is one of the earliest breeds developed in the United States. It's believed that Figure, the name of the very first Morgan horse, was owned by school teacher Justin Morgan, who lived in West Springfield, Massachusetts in the late 1700s. Someone gave the beautiful, little stallion to Justin for payment of a debt.

When Justin decided to enter Figure in a race, the man soon discovered his new horse could beat all others in any race. Justin had no idea what breeds comprised the lineage of Figure, but some folks assumed the horse had Dutch Friesian, Arabian, and Thoroughbred in him.

The importance of the Morgan horse in the history and development of many other breeds in America cannot be overemphasized. When Justin started to breed Figure, a line of excellent carriage horses, plow horses, and Pony Express mounts developed. All through the 1800s, Morgans also served as coach horses, for harness racing, and for trail riding. They also served as cavalry horses for the North and the South during the American Civil War, as mounts for pioneers going west, and for miners in the Gold Rush in California in the mid-1800s.

If you study the lineage of other major American breeds including the American Quarter Horse, Standardbred, The Missouri Fox Trotter, and Tennessee Walking Horse, you'll find that the Morgan played a major role. In the 19th and 20th Centuries, Morgans found their way into other countries, including England, where a Morgan stallion became one of the foundation sires of the Hackney.

The Morgan is a handsome yet strong and muscular horse with a gorgeous thick, arched neck. He stands between 14.1 and 15.2 hands and comes in most colors including palomino and even some pinto, although multi-colored ones are rare. His popularity over the last two centuries centers on the strong foundation the first Morgan built, which led to a breed with many skills. Today he's shown in all kinds of English and western shows, including western pleasure, dressage, show jumping, and endurance riding. He can be seen in driving competitions, including combined driving, carriage driving, and trail riding.

But there's more! Because of their gentle nature and steady gaits, Morgans are often safe mounts for kids in 4-H and Pony Clubs. They're also safe therapeutic animals due to their calm disposition and easy strides. Morgans are certainly versatile…and popular. They're so popular that two states, Vermont and Massachusetts, have made the Morgan their state animal.

Although Figure had a reputation as an excellent breeding stallion, there are records for only six of his male offspring, and only three of those were known as foundation sires for the breed. However, the breed is so popular, Morgan-only shows are held throughout the U.S. In 1973, the first annual Grand National and World Championship Morgan Horse Show opened in Detroit, Michigan. In 1975 that national show moved to its present home in Oklahoma City, Oklahoma. Over 1,000 horses compete in that show every year!

You might have noticed the word "foundation" reoccurring as we learned about the Morgan breed. A foundation is a solid base or structure on which other things are built.

Figure became the "foundation sire" for an entire breed. Thousands of other horses have their roots in that amazing horse. But do you know we as humans have a firm foundation in someone? That someone is the Lord Jesus Christ, the foundation of our faith.

When Jesus came to earth and died on the cross for our sins, He made it clear He was the foundation of our Christian faith.

Without His sacrifice of blood on the cross and His resurrection, we wouldn't have anything to base our beliefs on.

Sadly, many people around the world base their faith on false gods made of wood and stone that can't hear, speak, or answer prayer. But we have a living God, who answers prayer and gives us peace in our hearts that we'll have a home in heaven with Him someday.

If you believe in Jesus as your Savior, you have the best foundation you could ever have. With the Bible as your "behavior guide" and God's promise of heaven someday, there's no reason to ever doubt the salvation Jesus has given to you.

PRAYER:

Dear God, I thank Jesus for being my Savior and being the foundation of my faith. I can always trust in Him and His Word, the Bible. In Jesus' name, amen.

SADDLE UP! (What would God have you do now?)

Write how Jesus has become the foundation in your Christian life:

_____

_____

Take your ride: (Do you know?)

Figure lived until 1821 when, sadly, he was kicked by another horse and later died from his injuries. He was buried in Tunbridge, Vermont.

Dismount and cool down your horse! (Do you know?)

"Of old hast thou laid the foundation of the earth: and the heavens are the work of thy hands" (Psalm 102: 25).

Day 41

The Mustang: A Tongue Bridled and Tamed

"...We put bits in horses' mouths that they may obey us,
and we turn their whole body.
Even so the tongue is a little member and boasts great things.
See how great a forest a little fire kindles!"
(James 3:3, 5 NKJV)

"Mustang" refers to the wild horses that roam the ranges of the western United States. The name comes from the Spanish word mesteña, which means "wild" or "stray."

If you want to know what a Mustang looks like, that's hard to describe because the breed has no overall characteristics. The reason? Many different breeds of horses over the centuries have contributed to the Mustang's development. Some Mustangs are large and plump; others are smaller and delicate. The amount of available forage in different ranges also contributes to the horses' different body shapes and sizes.

Although Mustangs are considered wild, the proper term is "feral" because they descended from domesticated horses. Mustangs are a breed known for their sure-footedness, toughness, and intelligence. They range from 13 to 16 hands, weigh from 600 to 1000 pounds, and are well suited for the rugged land. Mustangs come in any color or combination of colors.

Although Mustangs are often referred to as an "Indian ponies" or "paint ponies," they're not ponies but horses. Strangely, Native Americans were not the first to own Mustangs. In the 16th Century, Spanish conquistadors arrived in America with their equines that had Barb and Iberian roots. When the Native Americans realized how useful horses could be, they embraced them and made them an important part of their culture. Over time, large bands of wild horses formed in the West from those abandoned or those that escaped and ran free from the Native Americans, Spanish explorers, ranchers, soldiers, and miners. From those horses came Mustangs numbering between two and four million in the mid-17th Century. However, over the next three hundred years, the numbers reduced drastically from either natural causes or ranchers shooting the Mustangs to protect grazing lands. It took until near the end of the 20th Century for anything to be done to keep the Mustangs from going extinct.

Finally, Mustang enthusiasts and horse lovers in general decided to protect the magnificent Mustangs that are a symbol of America's pioneer spirit of the Wild West. In 1971, Congress passed the Wild Free-Roaming Horse and Burro Act. With that bill, the Bureau of Land Management (BLM) became responsible for preserving and managing the wild Mustangs and keeping an eye on the ecological balance between wild horse herds, wildlife, and domestic animals grazing on western public lands. Today the number of wild Mustangs is believed to be at least 50,000.

Although Mustang enthusiasts believe all Mustangs should roam free, an alternative plan developed to save the herds from dying off or being killed. To help control the overpopulation of Mustangs, cowboys rounded up some of the horses and placed them in temporary holding areas or offered them to be adopted by horse lovers. This plan is still in effect today. But the one thing Mustang advocates are dead set against is selling the horses for their meat to dog food suppliers.

The BLM determines where and how many Mustangs will be kept as free-roaming animals. More than half of all Mustangs in North America are in Nevada (which features the horses on its state quarter coin). Other very large herds are found in California, Oregon, Utah, Montana, and Wyoming. Yet, another 34,000 horses are in government-run holding facilities.

The National Mustang Association (NMA), established in 1965, works closely with the Bureau of Land Management. They help place Mustangs in good homes of horse-loving people. Thousands of Mustangs have been adopted by patient owners, who have gentled and trained them for trail riding.

Training a wild Mustang requires lots of time and patience. After the horse learns to trust his owner, one of the first steps is getting the horse to respond to the bit in his mouth. Once he knows the bridle is to help him not hurt him, the Mustang learns to control his whole body depending on which way his rider reins the bit. Although the bit is only a few inches long, it can make a powerful, spunky horse obey!

The Bible tells us that our mouths need to be controlled just like the Mustangs' mouths. Our words can get us into a lot of trouble.

Have you ever said something that was just plain mean or nasty? Do you lose your temper and lose control of your tongue? God wants us to know if we learn to control our tongues, we'll be better able to control our whole bodies. A sign of wisdom and obedience to God is learning to control our tongues.

So how is such a hard thing possible? The Bible says to think before you speak and always look for encouraging words to say. If you pray for God's help and focus on being positive, you'll learn to control your tongue and become a kind young Christian.

PRAYER:

Dear God, please help me control the words I say. I want to be kind to others. In Jesus' name, amen.

SADDLE UP! (What would God have you do now?)

What should you do if you say something unkind to a family member or friend?

_____

_____

_____

_____

_____

_____

Take your ride: (Do you know?)

The NMA has an Adopt-a-Horse-For-A-Year program. The Mustangs in this program roam freely at the Barclay, Nevada ranch owned by the NMA. This special place is a sanctuary for Mustangs and other wildlife.

Dismount and cool down your horse! (Do you know?)

"Do not be like the horse or like the mule, which have no understanding, which must be harnessed with bit and bridle, else they will not come near you" (Psalm 32:9).

Day 42

The New Forest Pony: An Unusual Mark

"But the fruit of the Spirit is love, joy, peace, longsuffering, kindness, goodness, faithfulness, gentleness, self-control. Against such there is no law."
(Galatians 5:22-23)

If you cross the Atlantic Ocean and travel to the area of New Forest in Hampshire, southern England, you'll find where the New Forest Ponies originated and still live today. For several thousand years, they've been known as one of the most recognized mountain and native equines in the British Isles. As with many pony breeds, New Forest Ponies started their careers as "pit ponies" in mines. Fortunately because of their gentle nature, intelligence, and versatility, they soon became a favorite pet outside the mines. Today the New Forest Pony and similar crossbreeds are still the folks of that region's favorite choice for getting a hard job done.

Although their height is only about 12 to 14.2 hands, they're strong, surefooted, hard workers and great for trail riding. Many of these equines are so strong, adults as well as children can ride the taller ones. The ponies also can be driven in harness competition and sometimes even win against larger horses. New Forest ponies also are used today for dressage, gymkhanas, show jumping, cross-country, dressage, and eventing (considered the most demanding of races for both horse and rider. It originated with well-trained cavalry horses, which had to cover rough terrain and obstacles while running at full speed.)

New Forest Ponies are usually bay, chestnut, or gray. They can't be piebald, skewbald, nor blue-eyed cream, and only geldings and mares can be registered if they are palomino or very light chestnut. They may have white markings on their head and lower legs, but they can't have white behind the head, above the hock on either hind leg, or above the knee in either one of the front legs.

What's so interesting about these ponies is they graze freely on the New Forest territory and are owned collectively by New Forest commoners. Those people, under the direction of five agisters (managers or caretakers), have specific rights to a certain section of the Hampshire pastures. However, the people must pay a fee to turn out their ponies to graze. In this "semi-feral" condition, thousands of New Forest Pony mares and a few geldings run loose most of the year. The stallions must be registered to keep the line pure and are turned out only for a limited period in the spring and summer during breeding season.

The success of this program is due to the agisters, who take responsibility for the ponies. Every year, they have a round-up and check each pony's health. Then they worm and "tail-mark" each one.

Tail-marking is the cutting of the pony's tail in a specific pattern unique to each agister. The tails are cut either in three jagged steps to the left or the right, in cuts on both sides half way up the tail, or with a cut half way up the tail to the right. By looking at any pony's tail, you can immediately identify the agister who cared for that equine and his region of New Forest. If you'd see any of these ponies, you might chuckle at the way the tails are cut.

The New Forest Pony Breeding and Cattle Society has been publishing the stud book since 1960. New Forest ponies have been exported all over the world, including to Canada, the U.S., Europe, and Australia. Many other countries have their own New Forest Breed societies and stud books. As of 2011, there were 4,604 ponies grazing on the New Forest. In 2014, the Rare Breeds Survival Trust (RBST) conservation group listed the New Forest pony as a minority breed because less than 3,000 breeding females were documented.

Regardless of the numbers of New Forest Ponies in the world today, they can be immediately identified by their tail markings. Those unique tails tell everyone the agister who marked them and from what part of New Forest they came. That mark or strange way of identification lets everyone know these proud ponies are from Hampshire, southern England.

Speaking of marks or identifications, can others tell you are a Christian by the "marks of the Lord Jesus" on your life?

If you're a Christian, you should have the marks that identify a Christian. Those marks are called the "fruits of the spirit": love, joy, peace, patience, and kindness are some of those marks. The Holy Spirit helps you develop those excellent character traits when you're willing to follow His commands.

As you grow in your Christian faith, those around you will notice the "new you," and will identify you as a young person with the marks of a true Christian.

PRAYER:

Dear God, please help me be willing to obey so that I can have the fruits of the Holy Spirit and have the marks of a Christian on my life. In Jesus' name, amen.

SADDLE UP! (What would God have you do now?)

List three fruits of the Holy Spirit (Galatians 5:22-23) and how you can display those "marks" to those around you. (Example: **Love** – I can write my mother or teacher a note, thanking them for loving and helping me):

_____

_____

_____

_____

_____

_____

Take your ride: (Do you know?)

If a pony fits all the qualifications of a New Forest, but he has blue eyes, he can't be registered.

Dismount and cool down your horse! (Do you know?)

"And whatever you do in word or deed, do all in the name of the Lord Jesus, giving thanks to God the Father through Him." (Colossians 3:17 NKJV).

Day 43

The Nez Perce (Nez Perz):
The Horse with an Attitude

"Finally, brethren, whatsoever things are true, whatsoever things are honest, whatsoever things are just, whatsoever things are pure, whatsoever things are lovely, whatsoever things are of good report; if there be any virtue, and if there be any praise, think on these things."
(Philippians 4:8)

The Nez Perce Horse is another breed with deep roots in the United States. This fascinating horse originated with the American native tribe of the Nez Perce, who lived in Idaho and are still recognized by the federal government as authentic Native Americans living in the Pacific Northwest today.

In 1805, when Lewis and Clark made their way through the Bitterroot Mountains into Nez Perce territory in eastern Idaho, they noticed the natives riding strong, magnificent horses. At that time the breed of horse was called the Cordoba, which resembled a breed imported from Spain. The natives rode the Cordobas into battle because the breed had exceptional war skills.

Over almost the next two hundred years, many native tribes and their horses disappeared in America. But not so with the Nez Perce. Surviving through time, those natives took special pride in their horses. In 1938, they started to breed their horses with the Appaloosa, and a beautiful spotted or blanketed horse emerged. In 1995, the Nez Perce Horse Registry (NPHR) program began in Lapwai, Idaho, cross-breeding their Appaloosas with the Akhal-Teke, the stunning "shiny" horse from Central Asia. The United States Department of Health and Human Services financed the program and worked with the Nez Perce tribe and a nonprofit group called the First Nations Development Institute, which promotes such businesses.

Thus, a new breed of horse now roams the Nez Perce reservation. Today's Nez Perce breed is tall and muscular with the amazing colors of black, golden, metallic, and palomino. He can also be buckskin and dark bay with a spotted blanket or patchy coat. This new crossbreed resembles the magnificent equines the Nez Perce warriors rode in the past, and the Native Americans couldn't be prouder!

It's been reported that the Nez Perce say their horse has an "attitude." But the attitude refers more to the excellence of the breed than the way the horse behaves. The Native Americans have done their best to follow the lead of their ancestors and to carry on tribe's tradition and legacy. Their horse's conformation is longer and leaner than other stock horses in the western U.S., with narrower shoulders, a longer back, and narrow hindquarters. They're often gaited, with a fast and smooth running walk, and they're great for endurance races, long trail rides, and jumping.

With such excellent characteristics, you might say the Nez Perce Horse has a very good attitude! How about you?

Has anyone ever said that you have an attitude? Attitudes can be good or bad. An attitude can help shape your personality. People might say you are either pleasant or grumpy all the time. What should a Christian young person's attitude be?

The Bible tells us that Christians should always be cheerful and thankful for Jesus. If you love the Lord and want to please Him, then you have the best attitude you could have. If you sometimes have a sour attitude, then ask God to help you be kind and considerate, and He will.

PRAYER:

Dear God, I want to have the best attitude so I'll be a good testimony for you in front of others. Please help me to be pleasant and helpful. In Jesus' name, amen.

SADDLE UP! (What would God have you do now?)

List a few things that might cause you to have a bad attitude. Then write what you might do to change that attitude:

_____

_____

_____

_____

_____

_____

Take your ride: (Do you know?)

In 1995, the Nez Perce natives acquired four Akhal-Teke stallions and two mares from the country of Turkmenistan to start the Nez Perce Horse Registry and crossbreed with their Appaloosa-type horses.

Dismount and cool down your horse! (Do you know?)

"Your attitude should be the same as that of Christ Jesus" (Philippians 2:5 NIRV).

 Day 44

The Nonius:
The Ideal Horse for a Safe Ride!

"The horse is prepared against the day of battle, but safety is of the
LORD." (Proverbs 21:31)

The Nonius (Nó ni usz) from the country of Hungary has his roots with Arabian and Turkish horses going back as far as the 16th Century. During the 18th Century, the Hungarian kings decided to crossbreed their horses with stallions from Spain and Portugal, which led to a handsome horse with a thick arched neck, a large but elegant head, and a short back. Because the aristocrats demanded a beautiful yet limber steed, in 1784, the State Stud of the Hungarian Royal and Imperial Court in the southeastern town of Mezőhegyes was founded to develop a strong yet beautiful breed.

At that time, history records that Hungary had about 1.5 million horses, 10,000 to 15,000 of them working in the cavalry every year. Although the kings and aristocrats wanted quick riding horses for their military, the common people looked for reliable mounts for hunting and for elegant horses to drive carriages. Those demands led to the development of three different breeds: the Gidrán, the Furioso-North Star, and the Nonius.

You might think the name "Nonius" is a strange name for a breed of horses. The Nonius is a breed named after Nonius, the Anglo-Norman foundation sire. He was born in 1810 in Calvados, Normandy, in France. His sire was named Orion, and, while sources differ on his breeding, he was either a Thoroughbred, a Norfolk Trotter, or a combination of the two.

Even as a foal, Nonius was considered ugly. Even today the breed is known for the heavy head with a convex profile called a Roman nose. He's generally dark in color, most of the breed being black, dark bay or brown, either unmarked lightly marked with white. He's muscular and heavy-boned, similar to other light draft and driving horses and stands between 15.1 to 16.1 hands.

During the 20th Century, the Nonius became a farm horse. Sadly, as with so many beautiful horses in the 1930s and 40s, World War II significantly reduced the breed. It's believed there were only 50 mares left at that time. And for a few decades after the war, the lack of use for horses in Hungary sent many to the slaughterhouse.

The Nonius exhibits traits common to heavy-boned driving and light draft horses: a powerful and arched neck, broad and muscular back, and deep, sloping hindquarters. Although he's one of the heaviest warmblood driving horses, he's known for a kind, even temperament and eagerness to work in harness and under saddle. An extra bonus with this breed is he's easy to keep.

The number of Nonius horses today is believed to be at about 450 mares and 80 stallions. The largest population is still found in the town of Mezőhegyes, Hungary, with other small herds in Romania, Bulgaria, and the Serbian province of Vojvodina. Regardless of where you find a Nonius, you can make certain, he's been well-trained and prepared to serve over the years and will give a safe, enjoyable, and exciting ride.

How about you? Are you "well-trained" and prepared to serve the Lord every day? Do you get up with a smile on your face and a desire to do right? If you know the Lord Jesus as your Savior, He's ready to help you as you read your Bible and pray. Then you'll certainly be prepared to face each new day and the challenges it brings.

PRAYER:

Dear God, I ask that you'll help me be prepared for each new day by reading the Bible and praying. I know I can be "safe" with you as my guide. In Jesus' name, amen.

SADDLE UP!   (What would God have you do now?)

Write the things that distract you from reading your Bible and praying. Then determine to set aside a special time each day to meet with God during your devotions.

_____

_____

_____

_____

_____

_____

Take your ride: (Do you know?)

Today the Nonius is bred by horse lovers passionate about preserving the breed and is used for farming, trail riding, and competitive driving sports.

Dismount and cool down your horse! (Do you know?)

"Hold me up, and I shall be safe, and I shall observe Your statutes continually" (Psalm 119:117 NKJV).

Day 45

The North Swedish Horse:
Not Enough Good Can Be Said About Him

*"To you it was shown, that you might know
that the LORD Himself is God; there is none other besides Him."
(Deuteronomy 4:35 NKJV)*

The North Swedish Horse is a small, heavy horse originating from ____?____ You guessed it: Sweden. Equine enthusiasts consider him a coldblooded draft horse, but he can also be a harness racer if his build is lighter. He also has an impressive energetic long trot, which makes him popular for that kind of racing. (In harness racing the horses race at a specific gait. They must trot or "pace" but can't canter— run fast. One driver reins the two-wheeled cart called a sulky.)

The North Swedish Horse's roots go back to his neighbor, the Norwegian Dølahest. (The Dølahest is a strong, reliable draft horse from Norway.) North Swedish Horses had been crossbred with other breeds until the 19th Century when the North Swedish Horse

Breed Society created its standards for a more distinct body shape for the breed. The society returned to the horse's roots, using Dølahest stallions from Norway, and in the early 20th Century, the society also introduced tough performance tests for all breeding studs.

Today, the line of the North Swedish Horse is strictly controlled with breeding stallions that are all thoroughly tested. To qualify, a stud must have a pleasant character, must be strong enough to pull heavy loads, and must be able to breed. The horse's legs and hooves are even examined by X-ray to test for strong legs.

Because the North Swedish Horse is so cooperative, he's very easy to train. Although his build is compact and hardy yet light for a draft horse, his strength and stamina outweigh his "dumpy" look. He's tough and spunky, but he's also known to be cooperative and willing to work, so the Swedes use him for farming, forestry work, and recreational sports like pulling and hauling. Being born and raised in the harsh climate of Sweden, he's known for good health and a long life.

With all the positive qualities of the North Swedish Horse, it seems as though we almost have a near-perfect equine that stands at 15.1 to 15.3 hands. The most common colors are solids: blackish brown, smoky, and yellowish black, but any solid color can be found. His dumpy body shape might remind you of an overweight pony with a big head, long ears, and a short, thick neck. His mane and tail wave thick and abundant in the wind. Yet, despite his plump build, he requires little feed and is a very active horse. A farmer might use his North Swedish Horse during the week for plowing but on Saturday enter him in an endurance race at the local fair. Besides this equine's reputation for being a strong draft horse and racer, his easygoing manner makes him a favorite of children. Not enough good can be said about this horse loved by children and adults alike.

Have you ever heard the term "not enough good can be said about someone"? Has anyone ever said that about you?

Do you know we can say that about the wonderful God we love and worship? We can't say enough good about God because He *is* perfect, and He's the only God. Can you imagine never making a mistake or never doing the wrong thing? He made the vast universe, and He made us. Now Jesus is preparing a special place called Heaven for all those who believe in Him as their Savior. That's how special our God is, and He's worthy of our praise and adoration. Thank Him today for being the One and Only Perfect God who never makes a mistake.

PRAYER:

Dear God, thank you for being the one, true, perfect God, who loves me so much. Thank you, Jesus, for making a way for me to go to Heaven some day and be with you. In Jesus' name, amen.

SADDLE UP! (What would God have you do now?)

List some things you notice in your life or in the Bible that show that our God is perfect and magnificent:

_____

_____

_____

_____

_____

_____

Take your ride: (Do you know?)

The North Swedish Horse is one of very few coldblooded breeds used in harness racing.

Dismount and cool down your horse! (Do you know?)

"As for God, His way is perfect; the word of the LORD is proven; He is a shield to all who trust in Him" (2 Samuel 22:31 NKJV).

Day 46

The Norwegian Fjord: A Distinct Appearance!

"Even a child is known by his doings, whether his work be pure, and whether it be right."
(Proverbs 20:11)

The Norwegian Fjord (Fē'ôrd) is one of the oldest and purest breeds of horses. It's believed he has his roots in western Norway for more than 4,000 years. History records the Vikings embracing him as early as 2000 B.C. In more modern times, Norwegian hill farmers used these horses, (often called ponies), as little draft animals for plowing and carriage driving. However, as with most horses of this caliber, the Fjord can be found in competition worldwide such as dressage, jumping, eventing, and competitive driving.

Although he's considered a mini draft horse, the Fjord has smooth gaits, not high knee action like many draft horses. Because of his smooth ride and a pleasant temperament, he's a popular riding horse. He's great with children and special needs folks at Norwegian riding and therapeutic schools.

Fjords range in size from 13.2 to 14.2 hands and weigh between 900 and 1200 pounds when full-grown, but that's not what gives them a distinct appearance. They're all shades of dun (tan), mostly gray and buckskin. But yellow duns are very rare. The breed standards accept five different shades of dun, recognized in Norway since 1922. He can have no white markings except a small star on the forehead. In 1982, the Norwegian Fjord Horse Association made a rule that stallions of any age with any other white markings than a small white star cannot be accepted for breeding.

But now we get to the really distinct characteristics. Some Fjord horses have small brown spots on their heads or bodies. These "Njal marks" are named after one of the foundation sires of the Fjord breed, who had such markings. Many Fjords have zebra stripes on their withers and legs. The hooves are most often dark but can be a lighter brown color on light-colored horses. The feet sometimes have feathering, but that's discouraged by Fjord breeders.

Next, Norwegian Fjord Horses have a black "dorsal" stripe that starts on the top of their heads (the forelock) then runs down through their manes and down the middle of their backs to their tails. Another unique characteristic is the Fjord's mane. Because of the dorsal stripe, the hair at the roots of the mane is dark (usually black) but the outer hair is white. Fjord owners usually cut the mane very short so all the hair stands up straight. Sometimes it's trimmed in a crescent shape to emphasize the horse's graceful, curved neck. Other times, the mane can be trimmed in different patterns to display the obvious dark stripe.

And that's not all! The Fjord breed's conformation differs from many other breeds, and you can instantly identify a Fjord when you see him. Besides his strong, arched neck, he has sturdy legs and a solid body with lots of muscles. He has large eyes and small ears, and with a flat forehead, his face then appears straight or slightly dished. In the winter, his coat resembles that of a teddy bear because it grows long and thick.

Do you agree that the Norwegian Fjord Horse has a distinct appearance, which makes him so easy to identify? How about you? Do you have a distinct appearance, which makes you easy to identify as a Christian?

Your appearance doesn't necessarily mean the way you comb your hair or the way you dress, although your physical "appearance" should be modest and God-honoring. Instead, the word can refer to your demeanor or behavior.

How do you act when things don't go your way? Are you stubborn? Do you throw tantrum fits? Are you bossy, especially to siblings or other family members? Do you have friends, or do other kids avoid you?

If your answers to any of these questions indicate a problem with your behavior, today can be the time to ask God to help you change. God is willing and able to help you with any problem you have. If you're a Christian, the Holy Spirit is inside of you, and He's always ready to guide you to your best behavior. All you need to do is ask.

PRAYER:

Dear God, please help me to have a distinct appearance (behavior) so that everyone around me knows I am a Christian. In Jesus' name, amen.

SADDLE UP! (What would God have you do now?)

Think about your behavior over the last few days. Were there things you did that you'd like to change? List those things here and ask God to help you change:

_____

_____

_____

_____

_____

_____

Take your ride: (Do you know?)

Fjord Horses have two-toned manes and tails. Lighter hairs are on the outside edges of the mane and edges of the tail, and darker colors are close to the skin.

Dismount and cool down your horse! (Do you know?)

"I will behave myself wisely in a perfect way" (Psalm 101:2a).

Day 47

The Palomino: Pretty as a Picture

"A word fitly spoken is like apples of gold in pictures of silver."
(Proverbs 25:11)

If you want heads to turn your way when you ride by on your horse, then make sure that horse is a Palomino! Above all other breeds and colors of horses, the Palomino is most likely the one that most folks look for at parades. This equine is all about color. Stunning color!

Palomino horses have a yellow or gold coat, with a white or light cream mane and tail. The shades of the coat range from cream to a dark gold. The darkest coats are called "liver" or "chocolate" Palominos. Palominos almost always have dark skin and brown eyes, though some may be born with pinkish skin that darkens with age. Some have slightly lighter brown or amber eyes. They stand between 14 and 17 hands.

No one's quite sure where or when the Palomino appeared in history. Myths and legends from several countries shroud his beginnings, although the golden horse with the ivory-colored mane and tail appears in paintings and in ancient tapestries in Europe and Asia.

It's believed the gorgeous Palomino breed dates back at least to the 1400s with her Majesty Isabella de-Bourbon of France, the queen who pawned her jewels so she could fund the expedition which discovered the New World. It's recorded that she kept a hundred Palominos just because they were her favorites, and she forbid any commoner from owning one. However, we probably should thank Queen Isabella for her passion because she sent a Palomino stallion and five mares to her representative in New Spain (now Mexico) sometime during her reign, and from there, the Palominos spread into Texas and California. Cortes also brought some of the queen's Palominos with him to America in 1519. Some of them, or their offspring, eventually escaped and contributed to the golden colors common in Mustangs.

Horse enthusiasts call the Palomino a color breed because his color is found in almost every other breed of horse. Quarter Horses make up about fifty percent of registered Palominos. Thoroughbreds, American Saddle Horses, Arabians, Morgans, Standardbreds, and Tennessee Walking Horses make up the rest. Therefore, the Palomino is considered a multi-purpose horse, admired for his beauty as well as his versatility and endurance. You can find him in ranching, racing, rodeos, parades, shows, fiestas, trail riding, and jumping.

The name "Palomino" comes from a royal family in Spain, the Palominos. While Palomino organizations describe the ideal color as that of a brand new shiny gold coin, a wide range of gold, tan, and brown shades are all acceptable. And because of their distinct colors, Palominos are extremely popular for the show ring and parades. Many horse lovers say, "Palominos are as pretty as a picture!"

Do you know what else the Bible says is as pretty as a picture? Kind words.

God's Word has dozens of verses that tell us how important our words are. Words reveal what's in our hearts, whether we have kind thoughts toward others or nasty thoughts. Words can encourage a friend, or words can hurt like a knife going into someone's heart. The book of James tells us that our tongue can be a blessing or can be like fire. How do you use your tongue? Have you ever said anything you wished you could take back because they hurt someone?

As a Christian, you should want to use your words to cheer up others. If Jesus is your Savior, He can give you the right words to say in every situation. Then you'll be known as a young person who is kind and tenderhearted.

PRAYER:

Dear God, please help me be a blessing to others with the words I say. Help me to control angry thoughts so they don't spill out of my mouth. In Jesus' name, amen.

SADDLE UP! (What would God have you do now?)

Think back over the last few days. Are there any nasty words you said to anyone? If so, write the names of people you might have hurt with your words. Then ask God to help you be kind enough to apologize to those people:

_____

_____

_____

_____

Take your ride: (Do you know?)

One of the most famous Palominos was Trigger, known as "the smartest horse in movies," the beautiful horse of cowboy star Roy Rogers. Another famous Palomino was Mister Ed, who starred on his own TV show in the 1960s. His real name was Bamboo Harvester.

Dismount and cool down your horse! (Do you know?)

"Let the words of my mouth, and the meditation of my heart, be acceptable in thy sight, O LORD, my strength, and my Redeemer" (Psalm 19:14).

Day 48

The Paso Fino: Strives to Please his Master

"A student is not above his teacher, nor a servant above his master."
(Matthew 10:24 NIRV)

The Paso Fino (Paah´-so fee´ no) is a naturally-gaited horse bred by Spanish land owners in Puerto Rico and Colombia, South America, who wanted an obedient steed with endurance and a comfortable ride that would aim to please. All Pasos have their roots with the Paso from Peru, the American Mustang, and other descendants of Colonial Spanish Horses. The Barb, Spanish Jennet, and Andalusian have also been interbred in the U. S. to produce the Paso Fino of today. But Pasos go back to the time of Christopher Columbus when it's believed he brought some of the horses with him to the New World.

The Paso Fino is a gorgeous equine, standing an average of 13 to 15.2 hands but strong for his size. He weighs from 700 to 1000 pounds, although it might take a foal five years to reach his adult weight. He has a Roman-nosed head with beautiful large eyes, an arching neck, a short back with strong withers, and a thick mane and tail. He can come in any color or combination of colors, including white, pinto, and palomino.

The Paso Fino name means "fine step." It's a perfect title for a horse that's prized for his smooth, natural, four-beat amble. This is a lively horse that has a pleasant disposition with the desire to please his master. The Paso Fino has three different dominant gaits, all dependent on how fast he's moving. But in each gait, all four hooves travel close to the ground while he's in motion. At whatever speed he travels, the smoothness of the gait ideally allows the rider to appear motionless with no bounce. And a smooth ride like that would please any rider. Horse enthusiasts consider the Paso Fino the smoothest ride in the horse world (although owners of Tennessee Walking Horses hotly debate that issue!)

The Paso Fino is a competitive trail horse with both speed and stamina. But he's much more versatile than that. He often competes in western classes such as trail, barrel racing, versatility, and team penning, and is very popular for trail riding and endurance competitions, driving, and gymkhana. No matter what this spunky horse is doing, he's got one goal in mind: to do the best he can for his master who is riding him in the ring or down the woodsy trail.

Speaking of doing the best for the master, have you ever thought about God as your Master? An old hymn entitled "Give of Your Best to the Master" reminds us that we do have a Lord who should be the King of our lives. Everything we say and do should focus on trying to please God.

A master is someone in charge…someone who has authority over someone else. Our wonderful God is the Master of the Universe; yet, he loves us and wants us to live for him every day to show Him how much we love Him.

Sadly, sometimes we decide to run our own lives. We think we know better than God and want to become our own boss. Going our own way away from God's instructions (the Bible) always leads to trouble.

As a Christian young person, if you love Jesus with your whole heart, then strive to please Him in all you say and do. Be thankful God is your Master, who will always lead you down a path that only has the best in store for your life.

PRAYER:

Dear God, thank you for being the Master of my life. I pray that I'll always let you lead me in the way that is pleasing to You. In Jesus' name, amen.

SADDLE UP!   (What would God have you do now?)

List any "paths" in your life that might not be pleasing to God (examples: not reading your Bible, too much video game time, sassing your parents, being unkind to family or friends). Ask God to help you walk down the right path and always look to Him as your Master:

_____

_____

_____

_____

_____

_____

Take your ride: (Do you know?)

Ladies who ride Paso Finos in parades often wear the "traditional" Spanish garb: a fancy hat, long brightly-colored dresses with layers of ruffles, and high black boots.

Dismount and cool down your horse! (Do you know?)

"Ye call Me Master and Lord, and ye say well; for so I am" (John 13:13).

Day 49

The Percheron: The "Diligence" Horse

"Keep thy heart with all diligence; for out of it are the issues of life."
(Proverbs 4:23)

The Percheron is a very, very old breed. It's believed it developed in the Le Perche province of Normandy (a region in France). Thus, we have another horse named after a territory where he originated. The breed came from Barb horses left behind by plundering Moors after their defeat in the Battle of Tour in 732 A.D. Over the next few centuries, big, bulky Flemish horses were then crossed with the Barbs and Arabians, and the Percheron emerged.

Fast forward almost a thousand years. In the 1800s, the French government began breeding Percherons for its cavalry. Although the Percheron was first used for hard work and for war, he also had great value as a pleasure horse. Over time, the breed began pulling stagecoaches and later hauled heavy loads on farms. The horse's numbers exploded, and in 1883, Percheron enthusiasts in France started the first Percheron stud book.

In the early 1900s before World War I, thousands of Percherons were shipped from France to the United States, but after the war began, France stopped shipping them to America. However, Percherons were used greatly in Europe during the war, with some horses being shipped from the U.S. back to France to help in the war effort.

As the breed grew in popularity after the war, Percherons accounted for 70 % of all the draft (strong "pulling") horses in the United States. As of 2009, around 2,500 horses had been registered every year in the U.S. alone.

Today the Percheron is known for his excellent draft work. Purebred Percherons are used to pull logs in forestry work and to pull carriages in parades. They also compete successfully in English riding classes such as show jumping. Horse enthusiasts have crossbred Percherons with Thoroughbreds, Warmbloods, and other Spanish breeds to create excellent sport horses, and today Percherons are even making their mark in dressage!

Percherons stand from 15 to 19 hands. Those from France are born black and turn gray by the age of three. American and British Percherons can be either gray or black. Although Percherons are considered draft horses, they seem to be much more energetic than other draft breeds. They're also well-built with large muscles and have a reputation of being intelligent and very willing to work hard.

As the breed developed over the years, the French prized their Percherons as coach horses so much they called them

"Diligence" horses (the French word for stagecoach). These equines had to pull a load with elegance and speed. Thus, Percherons also have the reputation of being swift on their feet.

Diligence in France means "stagecoach," but do you know what diligence means in English?

If a person has diligence, he's a hard worker and is persistent at a certain task. A verse in the book of Proverbs reminds us to be diligent or persistent at keeping our heart (or our thoughts) right with God because what we think often comes out in our words. Jesus wants us to always speak the truth with kindness, and that can only come from our thoughts being centered on God and His Holy Word.

Are you that kind of Christian young person? Do you read the Bible regularly, so your thoughts and words are pleasing to others as well as to God? If so, those observing you will say you are being diligent and that you have a good testimony.

PRAYER:

Dear God, I want to always have thoughts and words that please you. Please help me read your Word on a regular basis. I know that will help me with my thoughts and words. In Jesus' name, amen.

SADDLE UP! (What would God have you do now?)

After you read your Bible, think about the verses you've read and write how you can be an encouragement to others with your words today:

_____

_____

_____

_____

_____

_____

_____

Take your ride: (Do you know?)

Sadly, it's been reported that Percherons in France are sometimes used for food.

Dismount and cool down your horse! (Do you know?)

"I said, I will take heed to my ways, that I sin not with my tongue: I will keep my mouth with a bridle, while the wicked is before me" (Psalm 39:1).

Day 50

The Peruvian Stepping Horse: Willing to Obey

"If ye love me, keep my commandments."
(John 14:15)

The Peruvian Stepping Horse is best known by another name: the Peruvian Paso. North American horse lovers also refer to him as the "Peruvian Horse." Can you guess where he originated? If you guessed Peru in South America, you're correct.

But you might be thinking that we just discussed the Paso Fino two devotions ago, so should we be talking about a "Paso" again?

Although the names "Paso Fino" and "Peruvian Paso" are similar, the horses are not the same at all. The Spanish word "paso" just means "step" and is not used by itself to name any breed. Although the two equines came from the same breeds in the Old World (Andalusian, Barb, and Spanish Jennet), the Paso Fino and Peruvian Paso were developed separately for different uses. The

Peruvian is a little larger and does one extra step more than the Paso Fino.

The Peruvian Paso has been called the national horse of Peru because of the breed's roots in that country. Conquistadors from Spain brought the breed's ancestors to Peru, starting with Pizzaro's exploration of South America in 1531. The horse was further developed there without any crossbreeding with foreign horses. Over time, Peruvian breeders worked hard to keep the horses' bloodlines clean and not crossbred. They wanted strong horses that were comfortable to ride and easy to control. Over the next five centuries, the Peruvian Paso emerged because of the horse breeders' dedication to the cause.

The breed is medium-sized, more muscular than the Paso Fino and stands from 14.1 to 15.2 hands. He has the reputation of having a willing personality to obey and to learn quickly. Stallions have a broader chest and larger neck than mares; however, even though they're big and strong, the stallions are also known for their easy-going mannerisms.

Peruvian Pasos can come in any solid colors, but grays with dark skin are the most in demand. Although pinto colors are not desirable, white markings are acceptable on the legs and face. Their manes and tails are silky but very thick and often wavy.

The Peruvian Paso is a light horse known for his four-beat gait and smooth ride. Although the use for horses declined over the years, especially with the arrival on the scene of the automobile, the

Peruvian Paso managed to survive because of his eagerness to obey in all kinds of venues. He could travel long distances, work on sugar and cotton plantations, yet provide smooth rides for ladies and children on a pleasure ride. As of 2003, there were approximately 25,000 horses worldwide, used for pleasure riding, trail, horse shows, parades, and endurance riding.

Thanks to horse enthusiasts not only in Peru but in the United States and Central America, the Peruvian Paso didn't become extinct. This breed is so special to the people of Peru that the Peruvian government has protected it by decree since 1992 and has been declared a Cultural Heritage of the Nation by the National Institute of Culture.

If you want to describe the Peruvian Paso, you'd have to say he's a very obedient horse known for his good temperament and comfortable ride. Because of his willingness to obey over the centuries, the horse has been popular and protected by horse lovers in other countries as well as Peru. A well-trained obedient horse is in high demand everywhere!

Obedience is a very important trait to have in a horse. A stubborn streak in a horse means big trouble. If he's not willing to obey, he might be no good to anyone. A horse that refuses a bit in his mouth or kicks at a saddle cinch is useless, and he might end up as dog meat!

Do you realize obedience is a very important trait for Christian young people to have in their lives as well? Do you know anyone who has a "stubborn streak" and always bucks at the rules because he wants to do his own thing? A person like that is hard to like and usually is not a good friend. No one likes a disobedient or stubborn person.

How about you? Do your parents consider you an obedient child? I'm sure they have house rules for you. Do you obey them with the right attitude? Would God say you're an obedient Christian young person? Do you obey God's commands like reading your Bible, praying, telling the truth, and being kind with a willing spirit?

If you do, you'll be a happy Christian at home and with your friends. By your obedience, you'll show your parents, others around you, and God that you love them with your whole heart.

PRAYER:

Dear God, sometimes I don't want to obey my parents and follow the rules, but I know I should. I love you and want to obey you too. Help me to be willing to obey. In Jesus' name, amen.

SADDLE UP! (What would God have you do now?)

Write the people or rules that make it hard for you to obey. Write why you think you have trouble obeying. Then ask God to help you with your attitude, so you'll be willing to obey.

_____

_____

_____

_____

Take your ride: (Do you know?)

The Peruvian Paso is so valued in Peru, there are now laws to control the export of national champion horses.

Dismount and cool down your horse! (Do you know?)

"And hereby we do know that we know him, if we keep his commandments"
(1 John 2:3).

Day 51

The Pinto: Precious

(Remember: The Paint in Day Four's Devotion is a completely different breed.)

"For the redemption of their soul is precious, and it ceaseth for ever."
(Psalm 49:8)

The Pinto goes back as far as Ancient Egypt, where images of spotted horses have been found in the artwork. Archaeologists have also found evidence of Pintos on the steppes (large grassy plains) of Russia from hundreds of years ago. Later, spotted horses were among those brought to the Americas by the Conquistadors.

By the 17th Century, spotted horses were very desirable in Europe; however, the Pintos' popularity soon faded, and large numbers mainly from Spain were shipped to the Americas. Some of those horses were sold, but others were turned loose to run wild. Native Americans admired the beautiful colors of the wild horses so much, they domesticated and bred them. The white man continued to import many of the well-established and stylish European breeds, which eventually crossbred with wild Mustangs to develop a more attractive and bigger horse that could do hard work. That special horse became part of America's "Wild West" history, especially the handsome Pinto. The Pinto became something very precious to the tribes all over the territory that would soon become the western United States. We can thank those American tribes because the U.S. now has the greatest number of Pintos in the world.

Although the horse world considers Pintos only a "color breed," the Pinto Horse Association of America considers them a true breed. As long as a horse has as little as three square inches of white above the knees or hocks (ankles), not including any white on the face, he can be registered as an official Pinto. However, most Pintos have large patches of white all over their bodies. Although some Pinto registries don't accept draft horses or animals with mule in their blood, some others do. But no horse organizations accept Appaloosa patterns at all.

Since the Pinto is a color breed, he can be found in practically all other breeds of horses. Therefore, there's no need to mention a body shape or "confirmation." You can find Pintos from Miniature Horses all the way to Thoroughbreds. In fact, several competing color breed registries have been started to encourage the breeding of pinto-colored horses.

All over the world, splashy Pintos can be seen in horse shows or simply meandering down woodsy trails. The dark colors blended with the white on so many breeds have wooed horse lovers for centuries. From the time of the Native Americans to the present, Pinto admirers have considered this color breed precious.

Precious?

You might be thinking, *How can a horse be precious? My mother says my baby sister is precious. She said that about our puppy too.*

The word "precious" actually means valuable or something worth a great deal. It also means unique and should be treated with great care. Obviously, Pinto lovers do consider that breed precious!

Do you know the Bible uses the word "precious" when referring to your soul? Nothing is more precious to God than human souls. Because He wants us to live with Him forever, Jesus came and gave his life's blood on the cross to save us from our sins. The Bible also tells us that Jesus' blood is precious. Only His precious shed blood can save a precious soul.

PRAYER:

Dear God, thank you for considering me "precious." I also thank Jesus for giving His life's precious blood for my salvation. In Jesus' name, amen.

SADDLE UP! (What would God have you do now?)

Write several people or things you consider precious. Then write why those people or things are so special to you:

_____

_____

_____

_____

_____

_____

Take your ride: (Do you know?)

"Pinto" is a Spanish word for painted, spotted, or dappled (different shades of brown or black).

Dismount and cool down your horse! (Do you know?

"Forasmuch as ye know that ye were not redeemed with corruptible things, as silver and gold, from your vain conversation received by tradition from your fathers; But with the precious blood of Christ, as of a lamb without blemish and without spot" (1 Peter 1:18-19).

Day 52

The Pony of the Americas:
A Special Friend of Children

"Jesus ...said to them, 'Let the little children come to Me,
and do not forbid them; for of such is the kingdom of God.'"
(Mark 10:14b NKJV)

Here we have a breed of horse (actually, a pony) not named after a person or a region from where the pony came. And this breed is barely over 50 years old!

In the early 1950s, Mr. Les Boomhower, a Shetland Pony breeder from the state of Iowa, developed a special new "little horse." He called it the "Pony of the Americas" (POA). His beautiful stallion, Black Hand, started the breed. He was a crossbreed of an Arabian and Shetland Pony with Appaloosa markings. Then in 1954, Mr. Boomhower and a group of associations founded the Pony of the Americas Club and gave Black Hand the first registration number. A year later, twelve ponies and twenty-three other horses had been registered, and within 15 years 12,500 ponies had been registered.

The men who started the POA registry wanted to develop a medium-sized pony for older children and small adults. Besides that, they wanted a beautiful horse with Appaloosa colors. Blanketed patterns became the most popular, though some are spotted like a leopard or have roan colors (speckled with tiny white or gray hairs). It wasn't long until the founders discovered that most POA foals were born solid then changed colors as they grew.

The first POA breeders strived to have their ponies display the delicate features of the Arabian and the strong muscles and bones of the American Quarter Horse. At first, the requirement for the ponies' height was between 44 and 52 inches. (Remember, a yardstick is 36 inches.) But in 1985 a final change was made to a height of 56 inches. (That's no taller than 13.2 hands.)

If you're not too familiar with ponies, you might have thought that all ponies have Shetland in them. However, since the founding of the POA breed, the early Shetland blood has been almost completely bred out to try to eliminate the roly-poly look.

Today, the Pony of the Americas Club is one of the largest and most active horse breed registries in the USA that focus on children. POAs can do almost everything "larger" horses can do. At first, they had been used for western riding, but over time, they've become excellent in endurance riding, jumping, driving, eventing, and dressage. Races similar to Quarter Horse races are often staged for children riding POAs, and the times recorded come close to races for full-sized horses! The POA is an amazing durable pony capable of performing numerous tasks…and all just for children!

As the POAs were developed especially for children, so our amazing God has a special place in his heart for children. The Bible has many verses telling us that Jesus loves children as much as He does adults. When He ministered on earth, He never turned children away, even when his disciples were annoyed by the little ones who wanted to be close to Him.

Do you know that you have a special place in Jesus' heart? He loves you more than you could ever imagine. Jesus always has time to listen to every prayer you say and wants to help you with every problem you have. Thank Him today for loving you the way He does.

PRAYER:

Dear God, thank you for Jesus, who loves me so much and wants to bless my life. Help me to love you and live for you every day. In Jesus' name, amen.

SADDLE UP! (What would God have you do now?)

Write a few things you can do every day to show Jesus you love him:

_____

_____

_____

_____

_____

_____

Take your ride: (Do you know?)

The Pony of the Americas Club has registered over 50,000 ponies.

Dismount and cool down your horse! (Do you know?)

"Whoever receives one little child like this in My name receives Me" *(Matthew 18:5 NKJV).*

Day 53

Przewalski's Horse: Saved!

"Therefore He is also able to save to the uttermost those who come to God through Him, since He always lives to make intercession for them."
(Hebrews 7:25 NKJV)

The Przewalski's Horse, (shə-VAL-skee) or Dzungarian horse, is a rare wild horse found in the steppes (grasslands) of Mongolia in central Asia. We can thank several men over the last few hundred years for discovering this unusual horse.

In the 15th Century, Johann Schiltberger, a prisoner of the Mongol Khan, recorded one of the first sightings of the horses in the journal of his trip to Mongolia. Next, Nikolai Przewalski, a Russian colonel, explorer, and naturalist, first described the horse way back in 1881, after having gone on an expedition to find it. In 1900, Carl Hagenbeck captured many of those same horses and placed them in zoos around the world.

Most "wild" horses today, such as the American Mustang or the Australian Brumby, are feral horses that came from domesticated animals that had escaped and adapted to life in the wild. However, the Przewalski's horse remains the only true "wild" horse in the world today.

Przewalski mares give birth at the age of three and carry their foals for 11 to 12 months. After the age of five, stallions look for mating partners. Each stallion creates his own group of mares or else wanders until he finds a group with its own leader. A big fight occurs between the two stallions until one wins the herd. The mares simply breed with the winner. After foals are born, like other breeds' newborns, they can stand almost immediately and can walk on their own.

By the end of the 1950s, only 12 Przewalski's Horses were left in the wild. World War II, zoological collections, and harsh winters all contributed to the breed's decline. Sadly, the wild horses in Mongolia also died out in the 1960s. The last herd was sighted in 1967 and the last individual horse in 1969. The species had been designated "extinct in the wild" for over 30 years.

In 1977, Jan and Inge Bouman founded the Foundation for the Preservation and Protection of the Przewalski Horse in Rotterdam, the Netherlands. Their foundation started a program to exchange a few horses found in zoos throughout the world to reduce inbreeding. Later the Bouman foundation began a breeding program of its own.

With so few Przewalski Horses left, horse enthusiasts rescued from 12 to 15 of them then reintroduced them back to their native land at the Khustain Nuruu National Park, Takhin Tal Nature

Reserve, and Khomiin Tal all in Mongolia. It's believed there are about 300 free and protected there today.

From that time until today, a joint effort by several countries has helped to save the Przewalski's Horse. Horse researchers, breeders, and zoo keepers have worked together in Mongolia, the Ukraine, Czechoslovakia, Hungary, and even in North America to preserve the special breed. The reintroduced horses successfully reproduced under careful management, and the status of the animal was changed from "extinct in the wild" to "endangered" in 2005.

One of the most impressive programs to save this special breed occurred in China in 1985 with the start of the Przewalski's Horse Reintroduction Project of China. Eleven wild horses were imported from overseas, cared for, and bred in captivity. After more than two decades, the Xinjiang Wild Horse Breeding Centre had bred many horses, of which 55 were released into a mountainous area. The animals adapted well and kept increasing. As of 2013, the center hosted 127 horses. They were divided into 13 breeding herds and three all-male herds, which are still thriving.

When the Przewalski's Horse is mentioned, it's good to remember that the breed would not even be in existence if it weren't for horse lovers around the world who have worked for decades to save it. Saving the Przewalski's Horse became a life-long goal of many horse lovers. Their dedication has paid off.

Speaking of "saving" the Przewalski's Horse, do you know our wonderful God has a "goal" in eternity to "save" us?

Maybe you've never heard the term "to be saved," and you might not know what that means. As usual, the Bible has the answer.

God's Word has many verses that mention "being saved." It simply means that when someone accepts Jesus has his Savior, that person is "saved" from their penalty of sin and will live with God in heaven forever. The Bible also says that someone only has to ever ask to be saved one time, and God writes his name in the Lamb's Book of Life.

Have you ever been saved? Have you asked Jesus, "the Savior," to clean your heart from sin and make you ready for heaven when you die? If not, there's no better time than right now.

PRAYER:

Dear Jesus, please come into my life, clean up all my sins, and save me. From this day on, I want to live for you. Thank you for being my Savior. In your name I pray, amen.

SADDLE UP! (What would God have you do now?)

Write today's date if you asked Jesus to save you. If you've done this earlier, do you know where and when? Perhaps one of your parents can help you with those details. Write them here:

_____

_____

_____

_____

_____

_____

Take your ride: (Do you know?)

It's believed the Przewalski's horse is the only wild horse that can't be domesticated.

Dismount and cool down your horse! (Do you know?)

"Neither is there salvation in any other: for there is none other name under heaven given among men, whereby we must be saved" (Acts 4:12).

Day 54

The Rhinelander/The Rhineland Draft Horse:
The Same...Yet Different

"For there are three that bear record in heaven, the Father, the Word, and the Holy Ghost; and these three are one."
(1 John 5:7)

If you do any research to read about the Rhinelander, you'll find there are two different horses named the Rhinelander. One is a classy show horse and the other is a chunky work horse!

The first Rhinelander, or Rhenish Warmblood, is a German breed registered with the Rhenish Horse Studbook. This beautiful breed is what you call a sleek horse and not dumpy or "square" in body shape. This handsome horse comes in all colors and stands at an average of 15 to16 hands.

This Rhinelander takes long, bold strides, and he almost has a bouncing quality with his walk, trot, and canter. Because he has a sweet and teachable temperament, he trains easily for any type of recreational or competitive riding. He's most known for showing in dressage and show jumping.

If you see a Rhinelander performing in a show, you'll find it hard to believe he once had been a heavy draft workhorse in Westphalia, Rhineland, and Saxony, all in Germany. As horses for pleasure became more important over time, the Rhenish Horse Studbook was founded in 1892 and focused on this Rhinelander as one of its specialty breeds. Then in the mid-20th Century, pleasure horses became more desired in Germany. By the 1970s, breeders began using lighter horses of the breed to refine this Rhinelander into a very desirable sport horse. To refine the horse even more, stallions from the Hanover-Westphalia area (western Germany) were used on Warmblood mares with Thoroughbred, Trakehner, and Hanoverian breed.

The second Rhinelander is known as the Rhineland Heavy Draft Horse. If you stand this fellow next to the first Rhinelander, you'd never think they are the same breed, but they are! This Rhineland Heavy Draft Horse averages 16 to 17 hands and is labeled a square horse. That means he's solidly built and has powerful, strong muscles, which enable him to haul heavy loads like logs and wagons full of hay.

This breed developed apart from the first Rhinelander during the last half of the 19th Century mainly for farming and other tough hard jobs. However, as modern times brought mechanization, this horse vanished from the world's scene as many other draft breeds did. It's estimated that in Germany alone, only 2% of all horses are drafts.

The Rhinelander Draft comes mostly in chestnut, chestnut roan, red roan, and bay colors. An interesting trait for this Rhinelander is his feathered feet. He has a well-shaped head, a powerful neck, and a muscular chest and back. The one similarity he has with the other Rhinelander is his quiet, willing, and energetic temperament, which makes him an excellent work horse.

It's interesting that two completely different horses are named "Rhinelanders." But there's something much more interesting about our wonderful God. Do you know the God whom we love is three different persons; yet, He is one?

Our God is known as "the Trinity," which means three-in-one. The Bible tells us that God the Father, Jesus Christ the Son, and the Holy Spirit are all the same, but they are all still different. Although it's hard to understand, we should remember to honor and worship all three persons in the Trinity. Each one has your best interests at heart and wants to help you every day in your Christian walk.

PRAYER:

Heavenly Father, thank you for also being Jesus my Savior and for being the Holy Spirit. Although I don't quite understand the Trinity, I believe You are the almighty God, Three-in-One. In Jesus' name, amen.

SADDLE UP! (What would God have you do now?)

Ask your parent if you can have a raw egg and a small bowl. Carefully crack the egg into the bowl and examine its parts. Often an egg is used to try to describe the Trinity. Look at the three parts of an egg: the shell, the clear liquid, and the yellow yolk; Then try to explain how it's "three in one:"

_____

_____

_____

_____

_____

_____

Take your ride: (Do you know?)

A trait both Rhinelanders have is strong, arched necks.

Dismount and cool down your horse! (Do you know?)

"Hereby know ye the Spirit of God: Every spirit that confesseth that Jesus Christ is come in the flesh is of God" (1 John 4:2).

Day 55

The Rocky Mountain Horse: "Watched" Carefully

"And to wait for his Son from heaven,
whom he raised from the dead, even Jesus...."
(1 Thessalonians 1:10a)

You probably think the Rocky Mountain Horse got his start in the Rocky Mountains in the western United States, but that's not the case. This special breed originated in the foothills of the Appalachian Mountains in eastern Kentucky in the late 1800s.

At first, Rocky Mountain Horses became the farmer's best friend. The equines pulled plows during the week and took the family to church on Sundays and picnics in the cool evenings. Doctors and traveling preachers also treasured this horse as a reliable mount because of his comfortable ambling, four-beat gait called the single-foot, which replaced the trot most other breeds had.

In the mid-20th Century, Old Tobe, a stallion owned by Sam Tuttle from Spout Springs, Kentucky, refined the breed as we know it today. For the rest of the 20th Century, Tuttle helped to keep the breed strong during World War II. After World War II, despite declining horse populations in the U.S., Tuttle kept his herd and continued to use Old Tobe as a breeding stallion. Tuttle also ran the Natural Bridge State Park business for horseback riding, using Old Tobe for trail rides in the park.

Old Tobe died at the age of 37, a very long life for a horse! But because of that one horse and his stamina, the breed survived and is now a favorite for competitive trail riding and endurance racing as well as working cattle. His comfortable gait and disposition make him a safe mount for the elderly and disabled, and he's also in high demand as a pleasure horse because of his good nature and ability to bond easily with humans.

The Rocky Mountain Horse can be any solid color with small facial markings and no markings above the knees; however, he's known for the preferred "chocolate" coat color and flaxen (blonde) mane and tail. He stands from 14.2 to 16 hands. He's also popular in mountainous areas for his hardiness and stamina during hard winters.

In 1986, the Rocky Mountain Horse Association was founded to increase the breed's numbers. Surprisingly, there were only 26 horses in the first round of registrations. Fortunately, because of horse enthusiasts, the numbers increased. In 2015, over 25,000 horses had been registered from the onset of the association, and the breed had spread to 47 states and 11 countries.

However, the Rocky Mountain Horse is still listed at "Watch" status by the American Livestock Breeds Conservancy. That means the estimated global population of the breed right now is fewer than 15,000, with fewer than 800 registrations every year in the United States. To increase awareness of this amazing breed, the Kentucky Horse Park hosts the International Rocky Mountain Horse Show every September.

Without the love and care of horse enthusiasts worldwide, the Rocky Mountain Horse would have passed off the scene. Because caring people are watching the horse's progress carefully, he's a beautiful breed that has a bright future.

Speaking of "watching," do you know as a Christian young person, you are to be watching for something very special?

The Bible tells us that Jesus is going to come for all those who have asked Him to be their Savior. On a certain day that no one knows but God, Jesus is going to meet all Christians in the air at the sound of a trumpet. He'll then take us to Heaven to be with Him forever. This event is called "the rapture." Until that day comes, all those who believe in Jesus as their Savior are to be watching and waiting with great excitement for Him to come.

Are you watching and waiting for Jesus to come for you?

PRAYER:

Heavenly Father, thank you for the promise that Jesus will one day come for me. I want to live for you and always be watching and waiting for that special day that will take me to Heaven. In Jesus' name, Amen.

SADDLE UP! (What would God have you do now?)

Remember to pray for friends and family members who don't know Jesus as their Savior. Write some of their names here:

_____

_____

_____

_____

Take your ride: (Do you know?)

A Rocky Mountain Horse with his rider can use the single-foot gait to go around seven miles per hour and short stretches of smooth ground up to 16 miles per hour.

Dismount and cool down your horse! (Do you know?)

"Behold, I come as a thief. Blessed is he that watcheth..." (Revelation 16:15a).

Day 56

The Sable Island Horse: Cared For and Loved

"Casting all your care upon him, for he careth for you."
(1 Peter 5:7)

What the Chincoteague Pony is to the Chincoteague Island on the Maryland/Virginia border in the U.S., the Sable Island Horse is to Nova Scotia, Canada. Sometimes referred to as the Sable Island Pony, this small feral horse stands no taller than 14 hands and is dark in color.

Sable Island is a crescent-shaped island about 190 miles southeast of Nova Scotia. It's only 26 miles long with sand dunes and wild grasses. Over 190 plant species and 350 bird species thrive there besides the herd of horses, which are the most well-known inhabitants. The herd is unmanaged and legally protected from humans. Sable Island and the Shubenacadie Wildlife Park are the only places you'll find these special horses.

The first recorded horses were brought by a Boston clergyman, the Reverend Andrew Le Mercier, in 1737, but many of those horses were stolen by sailors on passing ships. Most historians

believe today's Sable Island Horses descended mostly from horses seized by the British from the Acadians during the expulsion of the Acadians. (Acadian horses were descendants of several shipments of French horses, including Bretons, Andalusians, and Normans that later bred with horses from New England, including Spanish Barbs.)

Thomas Hancock, a Boston merchant and ship owner, purchased some Acadian horses and transported them to Sable Island in 1760, where they grazed in meadows. Additional horses were later taken there to improve the herd's breed. After the government of Nova Scotia established a life-saving station there in 1801, workers trained some of the horses to haul supplies and rescue equipment. Men patrolled on horseback looking for ships in distress, and the horses hauled lifeboats and life-saving gear to survivors of shipwrecks.

In 1801, life-saving staff recorded the arrival of a very important stallion, Jolly, who was probably similar in type to the original Acadian horses. Although Jolly wasn't the first horse there, he was the first to be identified in historic records. It's believed he survived until at least 1812. Other breeding stock, probably including Thoroughbreds, Morgans, and Clydesdales, were sent to the island during the first half of the 19th Century to improve the breed and raise the price for which they could be sold on the mainland.

The herd increased so much that, sadly, they were rounded up for private use and for slaughter (used for dog food), which by the 1950s had placed the horses on the "danger of extinction" list. But school children began a public campaign to save the horses, and it paid off!

In 1960, as part of the Canadian Shipping Act, the government declared the horses protected and no longer able to be rounded up and sold. Even today, the law requires people to obtain written permission before they can have anything to do with the Sable Island Horses.

In 2008, the horses were declared the official horse of Nova Scotia, and in 2011, the island was declared the Sable Island National Park Reserve.

Because the climate is so harsh, horse enthusiasts worry about the Sable Island Horses' survival rate. The latest census recorded about 550 horses on the island, but researchers have noticed a fluctuation every year. One year 80 foals were born, but it takes a year to know how many of them survive the winters. Also, food and water are limited on the eastern side of the island, so the horses must paw the sand to create little pools of water. So far, they've managed to do that.

The Sable Island herd has been completely isolated from humans and other foreign animals, so they've never had to have antibiotics or veterinary drugs. These equines also have the trait of hardiness and don't suffer from invasive diseases, which helps them to have long lives.

Although these little horses are special to Nova Scotia, a debate rages today because they aren't native to the island even though they've been there since the 1700s. Some people think the horses should be removed, but biologists and wilderness societies want the horses to stay. They believe the horses are important to the ecosystem of the island and are fighting to keep the horses right where they've been for hundreds of years. Because of people's care and love for these ferals, the Sable Island Horses will not only survive but also will thrive.

As horse lovers care and love for these special horses, do you know that our God cares and loves each one of us more than we can understand? He loves us so much, He sent Jesus to die on the cross, so our sins can be washed away. He loves us so much, he also gave us the Bible and Christian friends to help us live so we can please Him and not only survive but also thrive.

Do you just survive as a Christian young person or do you thrive?

PRAYER:

Heavenly Father, thank you for your care and love for me. I want to please you so that I can thrive, not just survive, in my life. In Jesus' name, Amen.

SADDLE UP! (What would God have you do now?)

Read 1 John 4, verses 7 to 21. Count how many times those verses mention the word "love" and write the number here. Copy the one verse you like the most.

_____

_____

_____

_____

Take your ride: (Do you know?)

The pudgy Sable Island Horses are dark colors, but they can have small white markings.

Dismount and cool down your horse! (Do you know?)

"Here is how God showed his love among us. He sent his one and only Son into the world. He sent him so we could receive life through him" (1 John 4:9 NIRV).

Day 57

The Shetland Pony: Sweet or Sour?

"Do your best to please God. Be a worker who doesn't need to be ashamed."
(2 Timothy 2:15a NIRV)

When you hear the word "pony," do you automatically think Shetland Ponies? I think most people do because Shetlands are usually the ones giving rides to children at carnivals and fairs.

Shetland Ponies originated in the Shetland Isles, located 130 miles northeast of mainland Scotland. Although these animals are called "ponies," they're really the smallest breed of horses in the world. They've lived on the Shetland Isles for thousands of years, and over time probably crossbred with ponies imported by Norse settlers. Shetlands were also probably influenced by Celtic ponies brought to the islands by settlers between 2000 and 1000 BC. The harsh climate and scarce food developed the ponies into a tough, hardy breed.

Shetlands are short, intelligent horses with thick coats and chunky bodies. They range in size from approximately 28 inches (seven hands) to a maximum height of 42 inches (10.2 hands). These ponies have short legs; yet, according to some horse enthusiasts, they're the strongest of all breeds of horse or pony. It's reported they can pull their entire body weight, while most breeds can manage only half. Shetlands are often gentle and loyal, ideal for a children's pet. Because of their strength, they're used for riding, driving, and pack purposes.

Shetland ponies were first used for plowing and pulling carts that carried peat, coal, and other items. Then in the mid-19th Century as the Industrial Revolution increased the need for coal, thousands of them traveled to mainland Britain to be pit ponies. That was not a pleasant job. The little horses worked underground hauling coal, often for their entire and often short lives. Many horses never saw the light of day from the time they started to work in the mines.

Coal mines in the eastern United States also imported some of these animals. The last pony mine in the United States closed in 1971.

Today, Shetlands are shown by both children and adults at horse shows in harness driving classes as well as for pleasure driving outside the show ring. Besides giving rides at fairs and carnivals, they're also seen at petting zoos and sometimes are used for therapeutic riding. In the United Kingdom, Shetlands are also featured in the Shetland Pony Grand National, galloping around a racecourse with young jockeys.

Shetlands are cute animals with small heads, sometimes with dished faces, big eyes, and small and alert ears. They have long, bushy manes and tails and dense double coats to withstand harsh weather. They almost look like Teddy Bears in the winter!

These little horses can be almost every color including pinto. But they can't be spotted like Appaloosas nor be a light tan, although those colors are sometimes seen in Shetland-sized crossbreeds.

Shetland ponies are found worldwide, though mainly in the United Kingdom and North America. In general, UK ponies tend to have more of the original characteristics of the breed and are often stockier than those in America.

It's not unusual for Shetland ponies to live more than 30 years. Most have a sweet personality. They're also considered to have a brave character. But sometimes they can be very impatient, snappy, and unreasonably stubborn. In other words, they develop a sour attitude. Because Shetlands are so smart and so cute and cuddly, owners often spoil them. When that happens, Shetlands can become headstrong and disobedient. Unfortunately, those ponies never provide a pleasant ride, never serve their masters, and spend most of their time getting fat in the pasture.

Have you ever had anyone say to you that you have either a sweet or sour attitude? Are you sometimes stubborn like the Shetland? A Christian young person, no matter what the situation, should have a sweet attitude.

You probably can recall that several devotions have dealt with attitude. That's because your attitude affects so many facets of your Christian walk with Jesus.

How do you respond when your parent asks you to do a chore you don't like? What's your attitude when doing chores? What would your teacher say about how you behave? Do you have a sweet attitude about going to church and doing your regular Bible time with God?

If you have trouble with a sour attitude, maybe it's time to pray and ask God to help you be a sweet Christian. Your good attitude will affect your behavior and will bring peace to your family and friends.

PRAYER:

Heavenly Father, please help me have a sweet attitude when things don't go my way. I don't want others to see a sour attitude in me. In Jesus' name, Amen.

SADDLE UP!   (What would God have you do now?)

Ask your parent if he or she has noticed a sour attitude in you at all. Write when that's happened and determine to do better with God's help:

_____

_____

_____

_____

Take your ride: (Do you know?)

The average height of Shetlands is three feet, four inches. Unlike other horses, they're not usually measured in hands.

Dismount and cool down your horse! (Do you know?)

"Behold, how good and how pleasant it is for brethren to dwell together in unity!" (Psalm 133:1).

Day 58

The Shire: The Gentle but Powerful Giant

"Say to God, 'How awesome are Your works! Through the greatness of Your power Your enemies shall submit themselves to You.'"
(Psalm 66:3 NKJV)

The huge, powerful yet beautiful Shire horse traces back to an equine called the English Great Horse that carried knights with their heavy armor during Medieval Times. It's believed the Great Horse developed in England from Flemish horses taken there during the 12th Century.

During the 16th Century, the Dutch brought Friesian horses with them when they went to England to drain flooded marshlands, and those horses probably had a great effect on the Shire breed. As times changed, even in war, the Shire became more popular for farming and commercial trade. Over hundreds of years and into the 1800s, this big guy contributed greatly to the movement of vast quantities of goods shipped both to and from English ports.

With the 20th Century came the invention of machines and cars, which could have caused heavy breeds like the Shire to die out. But horse enthusiasts didn't allow that to happen, so for the last hundred years to today a keen interest in "heavies" has preserved the breed.

The first Shires were imported to the United States in 1853, with large numbers of horses being imported all during the second half of the 1880s. The American Shire Horse Association was established in 1885 to register and promote the breed. However, over the years until the present, the Shires' numbers in the world have fluctuated, several times almost becoming nonexistent. World wars and modern machines have greatly impacted the importance of Shires in daily life, but when Shire enthusiasts became involved, the breed survived.

Fortunately, in the 1970s, the breed began to revive due mostly to breed societies in the United States, Canada, Germany, France, and the Netherlands. By 1985, 121 horses had been registered in the United States.

With all the care to preserve this special breed, there's still much concern. The American Livestock Breeds Conservancy considers the population of the Shire to be "critical." That means the estimated number of horses around the world is less than 2,000 and fewer than 200 registrations are made annually in the United States. The Equus Survival Trust considers the breed to be "vulnerable" meaning that only 500 to 1500 breeding mares are alive today. As of today, the American Shire Horse Association has only 3000 registered Shires in the world.

Because of their magnificent build, Shires always draw attention, even from people who don't know much about horses. At horse shows, Shires often capture the hearts of onlookers as much as any other breed. As far as "practical" use, the handsome breed is used for forestry work and leisure riding. They're also known for pulling fancy brewery wagons in parades. (Clydesdales, not Shires, pull the famous Budweiser wagons.)

The average Shire has a Roman nose, a big head, a very thick neck, and a big barrel (belly). He can be either solid black, bay, chestnut, shades of brown, or gray with only white on his face and white below the knee. Besides a height of up to 18 hands, this big guy has the distinguishing trait of having feathered (very hairy) feet. Although he's so big, the Shire displays a willingness to work and is usually very gentle and eager to please. If you stand next to a Shire, you might feel like a peanut. That's one reason some horse lovers call him the "gentle giant."

Did you ever consider God to be a "Gentle Giant" in your life?

Our great God is the giant of giants. Although He's gentle, He's also powerful. He's so big, He made the universe, the heavens, and all that is in them. Can you imagine how big God is to be able to do that? Yet, He cares for each one of us and knows us better than anyone else. And although He's so big and powerful, He still takes the time to listen to each prayer we make and every concern we have.

Aren't you glad our gigantic God who rules the heavens and the universe still has time for each one of us?

PRAYER:

Heavenly Father, I know you are big and powerful; yet, you take the time to care for me. Thank you for loving me and hearing my prayers. In Jesus' name, Amen.

SADDLE UP!   (What would God have you do now?)

Thank God for being a God who loves you so much. Write some of the things you've been praying for. Our powerful God hears every one of your concerns.

_____

_____

_____

_____

_____

_____

Take your ride: (Do you know?)

The term "Shire horse" was first used in the Mid-17th Century.

Dismount and cool down your horse! (Do you know?)

" Thus says the LORD, your Redeemer, And He who formed you from the womb: 'I am the LORD, who makes all things, who stretches out the heavens all alone, who spreads abroad the earth by Myself...'" (Isaiah 44:24 NKJV).

 Day 59

The Tennessee Walking Horse: Protected!

"For thou hast been a shelter for me, and a strong tower from the enemy." (Psalm 61:3)

If you want a splashy horse that will turn heads, then get yourself a Tennessee Walking Horse.

First known as the Tennessee Pacer, the Tennessee "Walker" is known for his unique four-beat running-walk that has no jarring bump like a trot has. Horse lovers often call this breed the "rocking chair horse" because its ride is so smooth. While a trotting horse does a flat walk at four to eight miles an hour, the running walk allows a Walker to travel at 10 to 20 miles per hour. In the running walk, the horse's rear feet overstep the prints of his front feet by six to 18 inches. The longer the overstep, the smoother the ride. While performing the running walk, the horse nods his head in rhythm with his beautiful gait.

The Tennessee Walker developed in the southern United States in the late 18th Century. Farmers and plantation owners wanted a more comfortable horse to ride on their huge spreads. They decided to crossbreed Narragansett Pacers and Canadian Pacers from the eastern U. S. with gaited Spanish Mustangs from Texas. Morgan, Standardbred, Thoroughbred, and American Saddlebred blood also added to the breed.

In 1886, a foal named Black Allan became the foundation sire of the breed because of his beautiful confirmation.

Although the Walker has a solid build, he's still considered elegant. He has a long neck, a muscular rump, and strong back legs. He can be as small as 14.3 hands or be as tall as 17 hands. He can be any solid color or several pinto patterns. He's extremely popular with horse lovers because of his calm disposition as well as his smooth riding gait.

The Tennessee Walker has been at the center of much controversy in the horse world. Over the years, some Walker owners developed a horrible practice called "soring." This practice involved stacking pads and weights on the feet of the Walker to make him walk much more exaggerated and unnatural than his natural gait. In 1970, the Horse Protection Act prohibited soring practices that often caused horses to go lame in a few years. Since 2013, this form of shoeing is prohibited at shows in all classes governed by the National Walking Horse Association (NWHA), and the United States Equestrian Federation (USEF).

Although stacks and action devices are prohibited at shows sanctioned by the U.S. Equestrian Federation and some breed organizations, sadly, in some places soring still occurs. The controversy over this awful practice has led to a split within the Walker community. Criminal charges have also been brought against abusive owners, and more breed organizations have started to protect the Walkers from such abuse.

In 2000, the Tennessee Walking Horse was named the official state horse of Tennessee. It's the third most common breed in Kentucky behind the Thoroughbred and the American Quarter Horse. As of 2005, 450,000 horses have been registered with the TWHBEA (Tennessee Walking Horse Breeders' and Exhibitors' Association) and about 14,000 new foals are registered every year. You will find enthusiastic Walker owners all over the U.S.

Walkers have appeared in numerous TV shows, movies, and other performing events. A beautiful white Walker sometimes played the Lone Ranger's horse, Silver, and a Walker named Traveler at one time became the mascot of the University of Southern California Trojans.

Tennessee Walkers are shown in all different western and English classes as well as pleasure and fine harness driving classes, with grooming similar to the saddle seat horses. Walkers usually show with a long mane and tail, and in some performance, halter, and harness classes, artificially-set tails are permitted, which only adds to each horse's stately appearance in the ring.

We can thank Walker enthusiasts over the years for protecting the breed from the terrible practice of soring. Because of those horse lovers, we can enjoy watching Walkers without worrying about them being in pain when they perform.

Do you know our great God is also a protector?

Because God loves each one of us, we can count on Him to protect us from evil and harm. God is the greatest force in the universe, and while he keeps his eye on all his creation, He takes the time to care for those who love Him. Maybe you never thought of God as a "protector," but He is. You can rely on Him to be right by your side watching over you as you face every new day.

PRAYER:

Heavenly Father, thank you for being my Protector. I trust in you to guide my footsteps each day while I try my best to live for you. In Jesus' name, Amen.

SADDLE UP! (What would God have you do now?)

Thank God for being your Protector. Can you recall any times in your life that you know God did protect you from harm? Avoiding an accident? Healing you from illness? Write those times here:

_____

_____

_____

_____

_____

_____

_____

Take your ride: (Do you know?)

One of the horses that replaced the original Trigger (Roy Roger's horse) was a Tennessee Walker named Allen's Gold Zephyr known as "Trigger Jr."

Dismount and cool down your horse! (Do you know?)

"I will say of the LORD, He is my refuge and my fortress: my God; in him will I trust" (Psalm 91:2).

Day 60

The Zorse: Just Plain Wonderful

"Many, O LORD my God, are thy wonderful works which thou hast done...." (Psalm 40:5a)

A Zorse? Are you wondering what in the world is a Zorse?

The Zorse is one of many equine crossbreeds known as Zebroids, which has the zebra in his roots. The Zorse is the result of a zebra stallion breeding with a solid-colored mare horse. The foal looks more like a horse than a zebra, but he has stripes. As with his zebra father, the pattern of a Zorse's stripes differs from every other Zorse. It's also possible to use a zebra mare and a domestic stallion to produce a Zorse. However, that's not a common practice because owners of valuable zebra mares don't want to waste a year of their breeding life trying to produce a crossbreed when they could be producing a zebra foal instead.

The zebra part of the Zorse provides resistance to certain diseases and pests that usually plague horses. Thus, he's very sturdy and hardy. Although there are only three different types of zebras, there are almost 300 different breeds of horses, which means the Zorse can vary greatly in size and color, depending on his parents.

The Zorse usually inherits his mare mother's temperament, shape, size, and color. He usually has short, coarse fur ranging in color from tan to brown to black with a darker mane and tail, but that also depends on the breed and color of the mare. From his stallion dad, he inherits stripes that usually cover his rump and back legs but can be found on the rest of his body such as the neck and head. He has a large head with a long muzzle, pricked ears and large, dark eyes with long eyelashes that give him a cute, cuddly look. He has long and thin but muscular legs, and his hooves are usually black (sometimes white).

A Zorse can only be born when humans bring a zebra stud and horse mare together. That's because wild horses do not roam in eastern and southern Africa where zebras live. Therefore, almost all Zorses live in zoos or animal preserves around the world.

It takes 11 months for a Zorse foal to be born. Like either of his parents, the Zorse can stand up within an hour after his birth and, because of his incredibly long legs, can run in a few hours. Although the hardy Zorse can live more than 30 years, he is sterile. That means he's unable to reproduce another Zorse.

Like other equines, Zorses only eat plants in order to gain all of the nutrients they need. They have an advanced sense of taste, which allows them to sort through grasses and grains in search of their favorite ones. They eats grasses, herbs, and flowers as well as leaves, fruits, and berries from trees. Zorses usually won't eat poisonous plants but are known to eat those containing toxins when there's not an adequate supply of more nutritious food. And the Zorses' digestive system is designed to have food flowing through it almost continually, allowing them to graze nearly all day if they want.

The Zorse was originally bred in England and Africa in the 19th Century to try and produce a domestic horse-like animal resistant to diseases spread by the Tse Tse Fly in Africa The experimental breed became popular until early in the 20th Century and the invention of the automobile. During that time up until the 1990s, crossbreeding Zorses disappeared. But then horse enthusiasts became interested in them, trying to crossbreed zebras with just about every breed of domestic horse imaginable.

Have you ever wondered why you don't see zebras being ridden very often? One reason is the zebra has a different body shape than a horse, and it's difficult to find tack to fit. It's also a known fact that zebras are stubborn, moody, and very hard to train. Thus, few Zorses are kept today for riding as well because they also are extremely strong and can be aggressive, making them hard to train.

Nevertheless, horse lovers who have taken a fancy to the Zorse sometimes breed them to ride, but often the Zorse becomes a work animal or an attraction at zoos, circuses, and animal preserves around the world. In Africa, Zorses become pack animals, transporting both people and goods up and down mountains.

Regardless of how you might see a Zorse used, you must admit he is an amazing, wonderful kind of "horse." As the Zorse is a wonderful "creation" of man with crossbreeding, so you are a wonderful creation of our Wonderful God. The Bible tells us nothing is too hard for Him. With His power He created the heavens and the earth. What's more amazing is He has made millions and millions of people, and no two faces have ever been the same.

Aren't you glad we love and worship such a wonderful, powerful Creator God?

PRAYER:

Heavenly Father, thank you for just being "Wonderful." I know realize that you are the Only God who can give me a home in heaven if I believe in your Wonderful Son, Jesus Christ. In Jesus' name, Amen.

SADDLE UP! (What would God have you do now?)

Look up Psalm 72:18 and write it here. Then in your own words, tell why God is wonderful to you:

_____

_____

Take your ride: (Do you know?)

"Zetlands" are zebras crossed with Shetland ponies.

Dismount and cool down your horse! (Do you know?)

"I will praise thee; for I am fearfully and wonderfully made: marvellous are thy works; and that my soul knoweth right well" (Psalm 139:14).

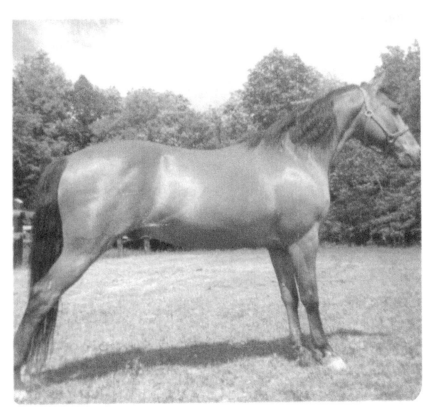

Rex squaring up

A PERSONAL NOTE FROM THE AUTHOR

Dear Reader:

I hope you've enjoyed learning about 60 different breeds of horses. I also trust that you've learned about our wonderful God and how majestic He is. But more than that, I pray, if you had never received Jesus as your Savior before, that you did so as you read any of these devotions. If you already knew the Lord Jesus as your Savior, it's my prayer that you now have the desire in your heart to serve God faithfully every day for the rest of your life.

Someday all those who've accepted Jesus as their Savior will be in Heaven with Him. The Bible tells us there are horses there too, and we'll get to ride them:

"And I saw heaven opened, and behold a white horse; and he that sat upon him was called Faithful and True, and in righteousness he doth judge and make war. His eyes were as a flame of fire, and on his head were many crowns; and he had a name written, that no man knew, but he himself. And he was clothed with a vesture dipped in blood: and his name is called The Word of God. And the armies which were in heaven followed him upon white horses, clothed in fine linen, white and clean" (Revelation 19:11-14).

Do you realize the Faithful and True rider is the Lord Jesus Christ? The armies are all those who've accepted Jesus as their Savior. We'll all ride white horses someday. Do you think they might be Albinos, Arabians, or Lipizzans? Maybe God is preparing a brand-new breed just for that special day when we all will ride with the Lord Jesus. I'm sure whatever the horses look like, they'll be the most beautiful sparkling white horses we've ever seen.

Please make sure you've asked Jesus to save you. Then you'll be in that glorious army some awesome day when we all ride together with the one called Faithful and True and the Word of God. When that time comes, and I'm riding my prancing white steed with a wavy mane and long tail almost touching the ground, I'll be looking for you.

Marsha

P.S. Can't get enough of horses? Check out the safe websites listed below

REFERENCES

WEBSITES:

List of horse breeds:
https://en.wikipedia.org/wiki/List_of_horse_breeds

1. American Albino http://horsebreedslist.com/horse-breeds/119/american-albino
    https://en.wikipedia.org/wiki/White_%28horse%29

2. Abtenauer http://www.theequinest.com/breeds/abtenauer/
https://en.wikipedia.org/wiki/Abtenauer

3. Akhal-Teke http://www.akhal-teke.org/tekes-in-sports.html
http://en.wikipedia.org/wiki/Akhal-Teke

4. American Paint
    https://en.wikipedia.org/wiki/American_Paint_Horse
    http://www.horsechannel.com/horse-breeds/profiles/paint-horse-horse-breed.aspx

5. American Quarter Horse - http://www.horses-and-horse-information.com/articles/american-quarter-horse.shtml
https://en.wikipedia.org/wiki/American_Quarter_Horse

6. American Saddlebred - http://www.american-saddlebred.com
http://www.asha.net

7. American Warmblood -
    http://horses.petbreeds.com/l/36/American-Warmblood;
    https://en.wikipedia.org/wiki/American_Warmblood;

http://www.horses-and-horse-information.com/articles/horses-hotbloods.shtml;
http://www.horses-and-horse-information.com/articles/horses-coldbloods.shtml

8. Andalusian - http://theandalusianhorse.com/The_Andalusian_Breed.html;
 https://en.wikipedia.org/wiki/Andalusian_horse;

9. Appaloosa – https://en.wikipedia.org/wiki/Appaloosa;
 https://en.wikipedia.org/wiki/Roan_(horse)

10. Arabian - https://en.wikipedia.org/wiki/Arabian_horse;
www.arabianhorses.org

11. Australian Brumby - http://australianbrumby.com.au/;
https://en.wikipedia.org/wiki/Brumby;
https://www.theguardian.com/world/2014/aug/20/-sp-a-time-to-cull-the-battle-over australias-brumbies

12. Austrian Warmblood - http://www.theequinest.com/breeds/austrian-warmblood/
https://en.wikipedia.org/wiki/Austrian_Warmblood;
http://www.equinekingdom.com/breeds/light_horses/austrian_warmblood.htm
http://equineavenue.com/site/horse-breeds/austrian-warmblood/

13. The Azerbaijan - https://en.wikipedia.org/wiki/Azerbaijan_horse;
http://encyclopedia2.thefreedictionary.com/Azerbaijan+Horse

14. The Azteca - https://en.wikipedia.org/wiki/Azteca_horse;
http://www.americanazteca.com/About_AAHIA.html

15. The Barb - https://en.wikipedia.org/wiki/Barb_horse

16. The Belgian - https://en.wikipedia.org/wiki/Belgian_horse;
http://ponynhorse.com/breed/Belgian%20Horse.html

17. The Brandenburger -
https://en.wikipedia.org/wiki/Brandenburger;
http://psi-auktion.de/eng/p.s.i.-auction/history/;
http://horses.petbreeds.com/l/111/Brandenburger;
http://www.mypets.net.au/brandenburg-horse-brandenburger/

18. The Camarillo -
https://en.wikipedia.org/wiki/Camarillo_White_Horse;
http://www.camarillowhitehorses.org/history_camarillo_white_hor
ses.html;
http://www.camarillowhitehorses.org/colts_fillies.html

19. The Canadian Horse -
https://en.wikipedia.org/wiki/Canadian_horse;
http://livestockconservancy.org/index.php/heritage/internal/canadia
n

20. The Caspian - https://www.caspian.org;
https://en.wikipedia.org/wiki/Caspian_horse

21. The Chincoteague Pony -
http://www.chincoteague.com/ponies.html;
https://en.wikipedia.org/wiki/Chincoteague_Pony

22. The Cleveland Bay Horse -
http://www.clevelandbay.com/about-cb-horses/content_-
_about_cb_horses_-_breed_standards;
https://en.wikipedia.org/wiki/Cleveland_Bay

23. The Clydesdale -
https://en.wikipedia.org/wiki/Clydesdale_horse;
https://simple.wikipedia.org/wiki/Household_Cavalry

24. The Curly - https://en.wikipedia.org/wiki/Curly_Horse;
http://www.horsechannel.com/horse-breeds/profiles/curly-horse-
horse-breed.aspx;
http://www.abcregistry.org/#/breed-standards/4553749480

25. The Furioso-North Star -
https://en.wikipedia.org/wiki/Furioso-North_Star;
http://www.horsedirectory.com.au/horseresources/horsesofworld/Furioso.html;
http://www.horse-games.org/Furioso_Horse.html

26. The Dutch Harness Horse -
https://en.wikipedia.org/wiki/Dutch_Harness_Horse;
http://adhha.org/adhha-breed/dhh-history-2/dutch-history/

27. The Falabella – https://en.wikipedia.org/wiki/Falabella;
http://www.imh.org/exhibits/online/falabella-miniature-horse/;

28. The Friesian –
https://en.wikipedia.org/wiki/Friesian_horse;
http://www.bonnieviewfarm.com/sjees

29. The Gypsy Vanner –
https://en.wikipedia.org/wiki/Gypsy_horse;
http://www.horsechannel.com/horse-breeds/profiles/gypsy-horses-horse-breed.aspx;
http://vanners.org/the-breed/

30. The Hackney Horse -
https://en.wikipedia.org/wiki/Hackney_horse
http://hackneysociety.com/meet-the-hackney.html#hackneyhorseanchor
http://www.horsechannel.com/horse-breeds/profiles/hackney-horses-horse-breed.aspx

31. The Haflinger - http://www.horsechannel.com/horse-breeds/profiles/halfinger-horses-horse-breed.aspx;
https://en.wikipedia.org/wiki/Haflinger

32. The Hanoverian -
https://en.wikipedia.org/wiki/Hanoverian_horse
http://hanoverian.org/

33. The Icelandic Horse -
    https://en.wikipedia.org/wiki/Icelandic_horse;
http://www.horsechannel.com/horse-breeds/profiles/icelandic-
horse-horse-breed.aspx

34. The Highland Pony – http://www.horsechannel.com/horse-
    breeds/profiles/highland-pony-horse-breed.aspx
https://en.wikipedia.org/wiki/Highland_pony

35. The Kentucky Mountain Saddle Horse -
    https://en.wikipedia.org/wiki/Kentucky_Mountain_Saddle_
    Horse
http://www.kmsha.com/breed_standards.htm

36. The Lipizzan - https://en.wikipedia.org/wiki/Lipizzan
http://www.horsechannel.com/horse-breeds/profiles/lipizzan-
horse-horse-breed.aspx

37. The Lusitano - https://en.wikipedia.org/wiki/Lusitano
http://www.horsechannel.com/horse-breeds/profiles/lusitano-
horse-horse-breed.aspx

38. The Miniature Horse -
    https://en.wikipedia.org/wiki/Miniature_horse
http://www.amha.org/
http://www.horsechannel.com/horse-breeds/profiles/miniature-
horses-horse-breed.aspx

39. The Missouri Fox Trotter -
    https://en.wikipedia.org/wiki/Missouri_Fox_Trotter
http://mfthba.com/
http://www.horsechannel.com/horse-breeds/profiles/missouri-fox-
trotter-horses-horse-breed.aspx

40. The Morgan – https://en.wikipedia.org/wiki/Morgan_horse

http://www.horsechannel.com/horse-breeds/profiles/morgan-horses-horse-breed.aspx

41. The Mustang - https://en.wikipedia.org/wiki/Mustang
http://www.horsechannel.com/horse-breeds/profiles/mustang-horse-horse-breed.aspx
http://www.nmautah.org/wildhorse.htm

42. The New Forest Pony -
https://en.wikipedia.org/wiki/New_Forest_pony
http://www.horsechannel.com/horse-breeds/profiles/new-forest-pony-horse-breed.aspx

43. The Nez Perce Horse -
https://en.wikipedia.org/wiki/Nez_Perce_Horse
http://www.buffalogirlsproductions.com/idahonatives/nez/horse.html
http://www.dreamerhorsefarm.com/nez-perce-horse/

44. The Nonius - https://en.wikipedia.org/wiki/Nonius_horse

45. The North Swedish Horse -
https://en.wikipedia.org/wiki/North_Swedish_Horse
http://horses.petbreeds.com/l/42/North-Swedish-Horse

46. The Norwegian Fjord -
https://en.wikipedia.org/wiki/Fjord_horse
http://www.horsechannel.com/horse-breeds/profiles/norwegian-fjord-horse-horse-breed.aspx
http://www.nfhr.com/catalog/index.php?aboutthebreed=1

47. The Palomino – https://en.wikipedia.org/wiki/Palomino
http://www.horses-and-horse-information.com/articles/palomino-horse.shtml
http://www.kurtzcorral.com/horseinfo.htm

48. The Paso Fino (Fee no) -
https://en.wikipedia.org/wiki/Paso_Fino
http://www.pfha.org/the-breed/breed-standard;

http://www.horsechannel.com/horse-breeds/profiles/paso-fino-horses-horse-breed.aspx

49. The Percheron - https://en.wikipedia.org/wiki/Percheron
http://www.horsechannel.com/horse-breeds/profiles/percheron-horses-horse-breed.aspx

50. The Peruvian Stepping Horse -
    https://en.wikipedia.org/wiki/Peruvian_Paso
http://www.horsechannel.com/horse-breeds/profiles/peruvian-horses-horse-breed.aspx

51. The Pinto - http://www.kurtzcorral.com/horseinfo.htm
https://en.wikipedia.org/wiki/Pinto_Horse_Association_of_America

52. The Pony of the Americas -
    https://en.wikipedia.org/wiki/Pony_of_the_Americas
http://www.kurtzcorral.com/horseinfo.htm
 http://www.horsechannel.com/horse-breeds/profiles/pony-of-the-americas-horse-breed.aspx

53. Przewalski's Horse -
    https://en.wikipedia.org/wiki/Przewalski%27s_horse
https://www.aboutanimals.com/mammal/przewalskis-horse/

54. Rhinelander or Rhenish Warmblood -
    https://en.wikipedia.org/wiki/Rhenish_Warmblood
https://www.usrhineland.org/about

55. The Rocky Mountain Horse -
    http://www.horsechannel.com/horsebreeds/profiles/rocky-mountain-horse-horse-breed.aspx;
    https://en.wikipedia.org/wiki/Rocky_Mountain_Horse
https://www.rmhorse.com/Association%20History

56. The Sable Island Horse -
    https://en.wikipedia.org/wiki/Sable_Island_horse
    http://www.cbc.ca/news/canada/nova-scotia/sable-island-the-wild-horses-history-and-future-1.2755142

57. The Shetland Pony -
    https://en.wikipedia.org/wiki/Shetland_pony
    http://horses.petbreeds.com/l/140/Shetland-Pony
https://www.britannica.com/animal/Shetland-pony

58. The Shire - https://en.wikipedia.org/wiki/Shire_horse
 http://shirehorse.org/ http://shirehorse.org/breed-standard-page

59. The Tennessee Walking Horse -
    https://en.wikipedia.org/wiki/Tennessee_Walking_Horse#cite_note-APHISfactsheet-25
http://ihearthorses.com/6-things-you-didnt-know-about-the-tennessee-walking-horse/

60. The Zorse - https://en.wikipedia.org/wiki/Zebroid; https://a-z-animals.com/animals/zorse/

GENERAL WEBSITES:
https://unsplash.com/search/photos/horses
https://www.biblegateway.com
http://www.horseworlddata.com/
https://en.wikipedia.org/wiki/Horse_pulling
https://en.wikipedia.org/wiki/Brandenburg
http://www.horsechannel.com/horse-breeds/
http://www.bing.com/search?q=scurry%20driving&pc=cosp&ptag=C1A68A4E9EB38&form=CONMHP&conlogo=CT3210127
http://www.bing.com/search?q=elborz%20mountains&pc=cosp&ptag=C1A68A4E9EB38&form=CONMHP&conlogo=CT3210127
http://scurrydriving.com/about
https://en.wikipedia.org/wiki/Gymkhana_(equestrian)
https://en.wikipedia.org/wiki/Csik%C3%B3s

https://www.youtube.com/watch?v=7xu7X4PJe58
https://en.wikipedia.org/wiki/Netherlands
https://en.wikipedia.org/wiki/Horse_harness
http://www.bing.com/search?q=Definition%20of%20dressage&pc
=cosp&ptag=G1486A68A4E9EB38&form=CONMHP&conlogo=
CT3210127
https://en.wikipedia.org/wiki/Guide_horse
https://en.wikipedia.org/wiki/Middle_Ages
http://www.bing.com/search?q=splash%20color%20of%20horses
&pc=cosp&ptag=C1A68A4E9EB38&form=CONMHP&conlogo=
CT3210127
http://bibleresources.org/names-of-jesus/
http://www.thefreedictionary.com/Rolls-Royce
https://en.wikipedia.org/wiki/Iceland
http://www.infoplease.com/encyclopedia/history/norsemen.html
http://www.bing.com/images/search?view=detailV2&ccid=p0pZR
yXQ&id=AD3000491216EBA0AC04C8A1AC67FC7DD018A7C
1&q=Map+of+Scotland+UK+United+Kingdom&simid=60805496
6941582757&selectedIndex=3&ajaxhist=0
https://en.wikipedia.org/wiki/Moorland
http://www.eriskaypony.com/breeddescription.htm
http://www.bing.com/search?q=Hapsburgs&pc=cosp&ptag=C53A
68A4E9EB38&form=CONMHP&conlogo=CT3210127
http://www.bing.com/search?q=centaur&pc=cosp&ptag=C6A68A
4E9EB38&form=CONMHP&conlogo=CT3210127
http://newforestcommoner.co.uk/2014/10/04/new-forest-unusual-
tails/
https://en.wikipedia.org/wiki/Nez_Perce_people
https://en.wikipedia.org/wiki/D%C3%B8lehest
https://en.wikipedia.org/wiki/Harness_racing
https://en.wikipedia.org/wiki/Isabella_of_Bourbon

BOOKS:

Edwards, Elwyn Hartley (1994). *The Encyclopedia of the Horse (1st American ed.).* New York, NY: Dorling Kindersley

Henry, Marguerite. *Album of Horses.* New York: Rand McNally, 1951

Henry, Marguerite. *All About Horses.* New York: Random House, 1967

Hubler, Marsha. *A Horse to Love.* Grand Rapids, MI: Zonderkidz, 2009

McHoy, Peter. *Best Loved Horse of the World,* London, England: Ward Lock Limited, 1979

Pickeral, Tamsin. *The Encyclopedia of Horses and Ponies,* Bath BA1 1HE, UK: Parragon Publishing, 1999

Ransford, Sandy. *The Kingfisher Illustrated Horse and Pony Encyclopedia,* New York: Kingfisher, 2010

Webster's New World Dictionary of the American Language, (2nd college edition). William Collins Publishers, Inc. 1980s

76984576R00163

Made in the USA
Columbia, SC
27 September 2019